Criminal Justice
Recent Scholarship

Edited by
Marilyn McShane and Frank P. Williams III

A Series from LFB Scholarly

Persistent Offender Law
Racial Disparity, Patterned Offenses, and Unintended Effects

Nancy Rodriguez

LFB Scholarly Publishing LLC
New York 2003

Library of Congress Cataloging-in-Publication Data

Rodriguez, Nancy.
Persistent offender law : racial disparity, patterned offenses, and unintended effects / Nancy Rodriguez.
p. cm. -- (Criminal justice)
Includes bibliographical references and index.
ISBN 1-931202-54-0 (alk. paper)
1. Recidivists--United States. 2. Sentences (Criminal procedure)--United States. 3. Preventive detention--United States. 4. United States--Race relations. I. Title. II. Criminal justice (LFB Scholarly Publishing LLC)
KF9226.Z9R63 2003
345.73'03--dc21

2003000398

ISBN 1-931202-54-0

Printed on acid-free 250-year-life paper.

Manufactured in the United States of America.

Table of Contents

List of Tables

CHAPTER 1

Crime Control Through Sentencing Severity

The connection between sentencing policies and criminal conduct has been the subject of substantial research and scholarly inquiry (Blumstein, 1996; Crawford, Chiricos, & Kleck, 1998; DiIulio, 1991; Tonry, 1996; Zimring & Hawkins, 1991; Zimring, Hawkins, & Kamin, 2001). As criminal offenders face a variety of sentencing schemes intended to reduce crime and forestall victimization, we are in the position of learning a great deal about the relative effectiveness of a variety of sentencing mechanisms. The high rate violent crimes committed by adult recidivists and by juvenile offenders in particular, has prompted the enactment of crime control policies directed at "incapacitating" serious, violent criminal offenders.

While such "tough on crime" initiatives are rather easily sold to the general public (Ellsworth & Gross, 1994; Gerber & Engelhardt-Greer, 1996), their ultimate true effectiveness as deterrents to the commission of crime and/or reoffending conduct remains uncertain at best. The implementation of poorly conceived crime control policies, of course, can result in a number of undesirable outcomes such as undue infringements of citizen rights, the generation of economic strains on offenders' families and support, and ultimately disenchantment on the part of the public at large.

The Nexus Between Three Strikes Laws and Theories of Punishment

Theories of punishment constitute the foundational basis for virtually all public policies directed towards crime control. Over the past thirty years, a shift from a rehabilitation theoretical foundation to a more punitive and retributive form of justice has taken place (see Blumstein, 1996; Cullen & Gilbert, 1982). Interestingly, while the criminal justice system is always experiencing strong pressures to reduce crime, it is nonetheless the case that relatively little attention has been directed toward acknowledging the actual reduction in crime rates observed over the recent years (Blumstein, 2000).

Despite a decline in crime rates across the nation, a persistently high level of fear of crime among the public prompted the statutory establishment of sentencing criteria for the more certain incapacitation of habitual criminal offenders in many states. As official state policy shifted from the previously favored rehabilitation ideal to more punitive, retributive and incapacitation–oriented models, the fundamental hope underlying public policy is that the tougher we get on crime, the less crime we will experience (Andenaes, 1974; Zimring, 1971; Zimring, Hawkins, & Kamin, 2001). While empirical research on the connection between punishment and occurrence of crime reveals little systematic relationship (Tonry, 1996), we nonetheless are increasingly likely to sentence juvenile offenders to adult criminal courts (Feld, 1987; Jensen & Metsger, 1994; Mays & Houghtalin, 1992; Sanborn, 1994; Singer, 1993), impose lengthy sentences for offenders convicted for drug-related offenses (Lee, 1995), and lastly, sentence third-time felons to life imprisonment (Clark, Austin, & Henry, 1997).

All of these "get tough on crime" polices produce substantial cost to the criminal justice system, and in many cases severely strain the resources of state and local government. Three strikes laws result in higher costs for incarceration since a greater number of offenders are required to spend the rest of their lives in prison. Of course, advocates of three strikes laws argue that in the long run many potential violent offenders are deterred from committing serious crimes by the certainty of severe punishment. Consequently, savings in law enforcement, prosecution, and court processes will result from three strikes laws. While available studies based on deterrence and recidivism tend to produce mixed and/or inconclusive results (Caulkins, 2001; Cheatwood, 1993; Fox & Radelet, 1989; Kovandzic, 2001; Marvell & Moody, 2001; Meehan, 2000), the widely held assumption remains that the threat of a possible life sentence will deter a substantial amount of future violent criminal conduct. The "eye for an eye" retributive notion of justice which is also the basis for this policy has the clear from opportunistic politicians who are well aware that crime is regarded as on of the most important issues facing most urban communities.

DiIulio (1995) argues that the reduction in violent crime rates recorded in recent years is mainly attributable to the toughening of sentencing policies that keep violent repeat offenders safely locked up behind bars. More certain sentencing schemes and longer periods of incarceration of known repeat offenders, DiIulio argues, serve well to prevent crimes that lawless persons would commit if they were free of these deterrent considerations. Thus, we need to identify systematically the victims of repeat victimization, identify the persistent offenders for incarceration, and support crime control policies of this nature across the entire criminal justice system.

The Creation of Three Strikes Law at the Federal and State Level

On September 13, 1994, President Clinton signed the Violent Crime Control and Law Enforcement Act of 1994 which provided for mandatory life imprisonment for persons convicted of a third violent felony. The sentencing policy feature of the act was aimed at the incapacitation of habitual offenders, repeat offenders, recidivists, and career criminals. Studies of the criminal histories of known recidivists provided some justification for the enactment. For example, Wolfgang, Figilio and Sellin (1972) had examined the official criminal records of 10,000 young males born in Philadelphia in 1945. Of the10,214 crimes committed by the group, more than half (51.9%) of the offenses were committed by 627 males within the total group examined (18% of the total group) (Wolfgang et al.).

A year prior to the Crime Act of 19994, Washington voters overwhelmingly approved Initiative 593, a ballot measure dictating that three-time "most serious" offenders be sentenced to life imprisonment without the possibility of parole (Stiller, 1995). The statewide initiative became effective on December 2, 1993, which amends Washington's Sentencing Reform Act of 1981 to define a new type of offense termed the "most serious offense," and establishes a new type of offender, the "persistent offender." A persistent offender is one who, prior to the commission of the present most serious offense, had been convicted on at least two prior occasions of any of the other most serious offenses. The county prosecuting attorney (an elected office) may charge the defendant under the authority of the initiative, and if the accused is found guilty of the offense charged, he/she will spend the remainder of their life behind bars in a state prison facility.

Initiative 593 defined "most serious offense" rather broadly, encompassing all Class A felonies,[1] including the attempt, solicitation, or conspiracy to commit any of those

---

[1] Class A felonies in Washington include: aggravated first degree murder; first degree arson; first degree assault; first degree assault of a child; first degree bail jumping with murder; first degree burglary; first degree child molestation; damaging a building, or facility by explosion with threat to people; creating, delivering, or possessing a counterfeit controlled substance; manufacturing, delivering, or possessing, with intent to deliver, narcotics; endangering life and property with threat to people; possession of explosive devices; homicide by abuse; first degree kidnapping; leading organized crime; first degree murder; second degree murder; delivery by someone over 18 of a schedule one or schedule two narcotic to someone under 18; possession of incendiary device; first degree rape of a child; second degree rape of a child; first degree robbery; setting a spring gun; treason; use of a machine gun in a felony (Revised Code of Washington 9.94A (21) (1994)). Initiative 593 specifically lists as "most serious offenses" the following: second degree assault; second degree assault of a child ; second degree child molestation; controlled substance homicide; first degree extortion; first degree incest; indecent liberties; second degree kidnapping; leading organized crime; first degree manslaughter; second degree manslaughter; first degree promoting prostitution; third degree rape; second degree robbery; sexual exploitation; vehicular assault; and vehicular homicide while under the influence of alcohol or drugs, or reckless operation of a vehicle (Persistent Offender Accountability Act. Initiative Measure No. 593, Ch. 1, 3). (1993).

offenses, any Class B felony offense with a finding of sexual motivation, and any other felony committed with a deadly weapon. In California, Governor Pete Wilson signed Assembly Bill 971 into law on March 7, 1994 and amended California's criminal sentencing scheme to include a three strikes provision. This provision provides for any defendant convicted of a felony in California who has two or more prior "serious" or "violent" felony criminal offense convictions to serve extended sentence lengths and possibly life terms (Stiller, 1995). Critics of three strikes laws have argued that the severe punishment of three-time felons is not only irrational from the deterrence perspective, but that it constitutes an overall "arational" form of punishment (Dubber, 1995). While irrational punishment tries but fails to advance the legitimate goals of state punishment, arational punishment exerts punishment without a rational basis. According to Dubber (1995), the passage of three strikes law represents our lack of regard for an effective policy that promotes public safety.

While three strikes policy proponents argue that the law is aimed at the most serious violent offenders, it was evident that early congressional proposals encompassed a broad range of criminal conduct, ranging from murder to minor assaults (Taifa, 1995). The wide range of offenses in the laws served as a reminder of how the public had becoming less tolerant of criminal offending. Still, the creation and implementation of three strikes law was surprising given the existing tough penalties built into federal sentencing guidelines and mandatory/minimum sentencing laws in place in most states.

While the public's fear of crime may be genuine, it is too often influenced by unreliable sources of information and unsupported empirical claims. The public's perception of crime may be inflated since perceptions, much like opinions are based more on anecdotal evidence portrayed by radio or television than on empirical data on crime (Stiller, 1995). Interestingly, in Washington State some defendants have avoided striking out by pleading guilty to lesser, non-strike offenses. In fact, the provisions of the initiative have been applied primarily against habitual robbers, even though the law was primarily directed at deterring and incapacitating sex, drug, and violent offenders.

California has experienced relatively minor non-violent property and controlled substance cases as third strikes. Lynch and Cekola (1995) found that among the first 100 three strikes cases filed in Orange County most defendants' third strike involved nonviolent crimes — mostly drug use and burglary offenses. However, most of these defendants also had a wide assortment of prior convictions for violent crimes such as armed robbery and rape. More recent research has found that three strikes law in California has had minimal impact on crime reduction and is utilized very differently by county prosecutors (Austin, Clark, Hardyman, & Henry, 1999; Meehan, 2000; Zimring, Hawkins, & Kamin, 2001).

The implementation of three strikes law has not come without challenges. Some constitutional challenges which have tested the validity of the law include following: 1) deprivation of liberty without due process of the law in violation of Fifth Amendment rights;2) Equal Protection Clause of the Fourteenth Amendment (creates two distinct classes of defendants, recidivists and non-recidivists); and 3) cruel and unusual punishment under the Eighth Amendment. Despite these challenges, the law has been upheld as constitutional (see State of Washington v. Paul

Rivers, 1996; State of Washington v. George W. Manussier, 1996; State of Washington v. James M. Thorne, 1996).

Some critics of the law claim that shifting discretion away from judges and toward prosecutors is inappropriate. In other words, this shift does not allow for the parole of recidivists, fails to evaluate the specific conduct underlying a defendant's charge, and leaves no room for sentence reductions for good behavior (Cushman, 1996; Feeley & Kamin, 1996; Stiller, 1995). Also, in order to cover costs of prolonged incapacitation, public funds from educational enhancement programs
and social services would be in jeopardy in the future (Austin, 1996; Stiller, 1995).

The Washington State Supreme Court did note that prosecutorial discretion has been limited under the initiative because the measure applies only to third convictions for a most serious offense.
While the public was instrumental in creating law that determined when to impose a life sentence, prosecutorial charging decisions may in practice result in either the release of dangerous criminal offenders by way of plea arrangements or the lifetime imprisonment of relatively nondangerous youthful offenders.

Research on three strikes law has also found minimal support for their cost-effectiveness (Caulkins, 2001). For example, some have found that most of the costs of imprisoning people older than 50 years of age comes from health care and related costs (Zimbardo, 1994). Older inmates tend to be less healthy than the general public, in many cases because of substance abuse in their youth. A continuous concern is that states with three strike laws will be forced to release first-time offenders in order to make room for the three-time felons. Critics of three strikes legislation have claimed that releasing young offenders when they have more of a criminal career ahead of them than older offenders is fundamentally illogical, and that this policy approach will not accomplish a reduction in crime (Austin, 1996; Burnovski & Safra, 1994). Also, policy analysts have predicted an increase in violence against police officers, correctional officers and staffs, and the general public as potential third time offenders encounter arrest, prosecution, and prolonged confinement (Taifa, 1995).

According to advocates of three strikes laws a substantial reduction in crime would be produced simply because known violent criminals would be in prison longer than occurs in our present system. To achieve a reduction in crime, three strikes laws would have to be implemented precisely as they are written (Greenwood, 1995). In other words, about one third of the felonies affected by full implementation would be violent crimes, such as murder, manslaughter, forceful rape, and assaults causing serious bodily harm; the other two thirds of listed offenses would be less-violent but still serious felony crimes such as less injurious assaults, robberies, and residential burglaries (Greenwood, 1995).

To date, a total of 199 criminals have been sentenced under the three strikes initiative in the state of Washington (Statistical Summary of Adult Felony Sentencing Fiscal Year 2001, 2000). This is a much lower number than the State Sentencing Guidelines Commission had predicted. Under this initiative, the county prosecuting attorneys are instrumental in determining who serves life sentences. Given the number of third strike offenders, it is clear that in a substantial number of cases, county prosecutors are choosing not to use the punitive provisions. Given the proportion of young males arrested for violent crimes, it is not surprising that three strikes laws heavily impact young male recidivists, specifically, African Americans. In the state of Washington, 46% of those sentenced as three strike offenders were minorities, specifically, 39% are African American. The state of Washington's African American population constitutes four percent of the overall state's population. Surprisingly, limited focus has been given to how three strikes laws disproportionately affect ethnic minorities (Taifa, 1995; Zimring, Hawkins, & Kamin, 2001).

In this study, I examine the advent and consequences of the State of Washington's Persistent Offender Accountability Act, a "three strikes" law. Primary emphasis will be accorded to identifying the type of offenders and offenses that have been impacted by this statutory enactment. This study will not only examine data containing all felony convictions committed in the state of Washington during a five-year time span (1992 to 1997), but will also rely on interview data from public officials who directly implement and respond to three strikes cases.

In the following chapters, a review of studies on the sentencing process will be presented. This discussion will include studies on courtroom culture, the development of sentencing guidelines, and legal and extralegal variables that have been found to influence judicial sentencing decisions. Attention will also be devoted to the creation and implementation of Washington's three strikes law. Combining research from criminology, criminal justice, and legal studies, theoretical models are used to examine the sentencing process of repeat offenders. Given previous research on sentencing enhancements, the sentencing process, and three strikes laws, a number of research questions are logically derived from the literature. After a detailed presentation of the methodology in this study, the research questions are examined and findings from these analyses are discussed. Lastly, policy implications based on the findings are presented.

CHAPTER 2

Sentencing Mechanisms and Courtroom Culture

Achieving the goals of sentencing policies is one of the more difficult challenges of democratic government. Providing for equity and justice in sentencing while protecting society from criminal offenders involves balancing quite diverse elements of justice. A comprehensive theory of criminal sentencing requires an effort to explain the causal links between criminal conduct, sentencing reform polices, sentencing behavior of judges and prosecutors, size and demographic composition of jail and prison populations, and trends in victimization. As such, studies on sentencing outcomes have suggested the assessment of court context to better understand judicial decision (Britt, 2000; Hawkins, 1987; Kleck, 1981; Kramer & Ulmer, 1996; Myers & Talarico, 1986).

Sentencing Process

Trend data show that from 188 to 1994, 45% of offenders received a prison term. This number actually dropped to 38% in 1996 but rose back to 45% in 1998 (Durose, Levin, & Langan, 2001). Even though elected officials are sensitive to increases and decreases in public support for greater severity and assurance of time served in sentencing practices, the judicial and prosecutorial elite within the criminal justice system remains directly responsible for the administration of criminal justice sentencing outcomes.

The major decisions that prosecutors and judges make in the course of their work have been the focus of various scholarly work (Albonetti, 1991, 1997; Crawford, Chiricos, & Kleck, 1998; Crawford, 2000; DiIulio, 1991; Forst & Rhodes, 1983; Hogarth, 1971; Kramer & Ulmer, 1996; Miethe & Moore, 1986; Myers, 1991; Myers & Talarico, 1987; Steffensmeier, Ulmer, & Kramer, 1998; Ulmer, & Kramer, 1998; Tonry, 1995; Zatz, 1987; Zimring & Hawkins, 1991; Zimring, Hawkins, & Kamin, 2001). Prosecutors decide whether and how to proceed with cases on their assessment of the evidence and the likelihood of a conviction under various charges. In this connection, efforts to curtail the powers and the discretion of prosecutors through judicial review of plea bargaining has received some attention Albonetti, 1998; Maynard, 1983, 1984, 1992; Alschuter, 1975). Whether and how to plea, when examined in conjunction with judicial review, raises interesting questions regarding the appropriate balance to be struck between prosecutorial discretion and judicial oversight.

Judicial discretion is exercised throughout a criminal proceeding, that is perhaps most obvious in the sentencing decision. Judicial autonomy is far from absolute, but is structured to a considerable extent by the types of cases brought before the court, the character of decisions made in earlier reviews of cases, and indirect community pressures. According to Myers (1991), courtroom decisions occur in "apolitical arenas," but extralegal factors may influence decisions. However, these factors appear in subtle ways (Myers, 1991).

Plea bargaining, most often recognized as a prominent aspect of the arraignment stage, is an essential part of the criminal justice system. While the right to a trial by a jury of one's peers is provided for in the Sixth Amendment to the U.S. Constitution, approximately 90 percent of all felony criminal defendants across the United States give up their right to a jury trial and plead guilty to a specific criminal offense (Walsh, 1990). From 1990 to 1998, we witnessed an increase in guilty please from 91% to 94% (Durose, Levin, & Langan, 2001). An incentive for both sides to bargain is based on uncertain outcomes that result in convictions of less serious offenses (Ruttenburg, 1979).

Most judges encourage plea bargains because they conserve often scarce court resources. Some have argued that the admission of guilt is the first step toward rehabilitation, and defense attorneys know that a guilty individual who insists on a trial may be viewed as troublesome and receive a more severe penalty than if a plea arrangement had been previously arranged. Other factors that may affect the probability of plea bargaining activity include inadequate legal advice or an attorney's desire to process his/her criminal caseload as quickly as possible (Uhlman & Walker, 1979). Interestingly, given the substantial probability of case dismissal, it is difficult to explain why criminal defendants are so frequently persuaded to engage in plea bargaining.

Eisentein, Flemming, and Nardulli (1988) examined sentencing behavior and plea bargaining practices and found that within seven jurisdictions, the average number of charges at arrest was 1.87. The average number of charges per defendant after the preliminary hearing dropped to 1.79. The authors concluded that after gathering information on arrestees, little changes in charges often result (Eisentein, et al.). They use the phrase "guilty-plea process" to indicate that guilty pleas do not always result from an explicit give-and-take bargaining practice. Instead, such pleas result from the defense side's accepting the established standard disposition, or the going rate (Eisentein, et al.). Thus, defense counsel accepts the sentence that forms part of the informal consensus on how specific defendants should be sentenced.

For most of the twentieth century, a system of indeterminate sentencing existed throughout the United States. However, a nationwide movement for the establishment of determinate sentencing, which began in the late 1960s came into prominences. This movement was rooted in two principles—namely, that the sentence imposed in court should reasonably resemble the sentence served and that post-conviction correctional system administrators should have little or no discretion over the duration of an offender's period of incarceration. Of particular interest to many advocates of reform was the issue of fairness and consistency for similar cases across jurisdictions. Specifically, the lack of equity in a system of courts wherein some courts maintained high standard dispositions and others maintained low structured dispositions was seen as clear problem.

As rehabilitation ceased to be the guiding philosophy within the criminal justice system, determinate sentencing schemes were intended to solve the problems not solved by the rehabilitation. Because determinate sentencing systems did not always succeed in resolving the disparity in case outcomes, sentencing guidelines were proposed and subsequently developed in many jurisdictions as either a substitute for or supplement to determinate sentencing. Thus, the "justice model" replaced rehabilitation as the basis of criminal justice processes (Cullen & Gilbert, 1982).

Sentencing Guidelines

Instilling greater determinacy in sentencing outcomes in American criminal justice institutions was also evident in the establishment of sentencing commissions. These commissions were created to: 1) contain corrections costs; 2) develop monitoring and assessment of correctional facilities in relation to correctional costs; 3) establish "truth in sentencing" by moving discretion with respect to duration of supervision and/or confinement from parole and corrections authorities to judges; and 4) reduce sentence disparity. The Minnesota State legislature created the first sentencing commission in 1978, followed by the comprehensive implementation of the state's sentencing guidelines in 1980 (von Hirsch, 1994). Federal sentencing guidelines similar to those developed in Minnesota have been in place since 1987.

Sentencing guidelines thus exist in many jurisdictions to establish a common rationale for sentencing, and to specify the major factors that should be considered by judges in making sentencing decisions (Clancy,

Bartolomeo, Richadson, & Wellford, 1981). The primary purpose sought by establishing sentencing guidelines was to make sentencing decisions more consistent and to introduce explicit policymaking principles into the sentencing process. Critics of sentencing guidelines, specifically mandatory sentences contend that because sentencing guideline statutes tend to be written broadly, many minor offenders, who pose no real danger to society are affected by "get tough on crime" legislative decisions (Tonry, 1996; Zimring, Hawkins, & Kamin, 2001). These dynamics tend to affect nonwhite offenders disproportionately, and thereby tend to hamper the racial/ethnic and class equity of such reforms.

According to Tonry (1992), mandatory minimums have tended to reduce defendants' incentives to plead guilty, reduced guilty plea rates, and lengthen case processing time. However, others have argued that states with sentencing guidelines have greater uniformity in their sentencing outcomes because decisions are based on the offender's role in the offense, acceptance of responsibility, and other mitigating factors (Schulhofer, 1993). Overall, they tend to achieve a higher degree of determinacy, predictability, uniformity, and severity than was the case prior to their establishment.

Even though sentencing guidelines have tended to curtail sentencing discretion to a considerable extent, some critics claim that sentencing guidelines still typically contain considerable flexibility for the exercise of judicial discretion. The most widely recognized avenue of judicial flexibility is the sentencing judge's ability to depart from the prescribed sentencing range. In the late 1980s the frequency of incidence of violent and drug-related crimes increased significantly and this development called into question the efficacy of the states' sentencing guidelines given the role of legal and extralegal factors in sentencing decisions (von Hirsch & Greene, 1993). Interestingly, studies on sentencing departures have found that both racial/ethnic and legal criteria are responsible for such departures (Moore & Miethe, 1986; Kramer & Steffensmeier, 1993; Kramer & Ulmer, 1996; Steffensmeier & Demuth, 2000).

Legal Criteria in Sentencing Decisions

An offender's criminal history plays quite an important role in the sentencing process in virtually all jurisdictions. Statutory enhancements for repeat offenders exist in most American counties, where there is widespread public support for harsher penalties. State and federal sentencing guideline systems in the United States attach a great deal of importance to criminal history information, but there remains considerable diversity in the way sentencing guideline systems define and limit the use of previous criminal convictions (Roberts, 1997). In fact, recent sentencing research has attempted to identify the most appropriate legal variables to use in predicting judicial decisions (see Engen & Gainey, 2000; Ulmer, 2000). Kramer and Ulmer (1996) analyzed sentencing data from Pennsylvania for 1985-87 and 1990-91 to determine the extent to which sentences departed from the state's established sentencing guidelines. They used a combination of legal, extralegal, and county factors as predictors of judicial departure. Results indicated that legally prescribed factors such as nature of offense and severity of the criminal history record were the main factors underlying decisions to depart from the guidelines.

Also, data from federal pre-sentence reports found that judges give stiffer penalties to offenders who commit more serious crimes, have more extensive criminal histories, and do not plead guilty (Frost and Rhodes, 1982).

Talarico (1979) examined an array of case processing variables and found that defendants who were detained prior to sentencing were more likely to receive prison sentences than those who were released on bail. Also, defendants who refuse to plea bargain received more severe sentences than those that plead guilty, and defendants with extensive criminal histories involving violence against others tended to receive the longest sentences. While under sentencing guidelines, legal criteria should be the guiding factor in determining sentence severity, research has found that both legal *and* racial/ethnic factors influence the sentencing process (Albonetti, 1991, 1997; Crawford, Chiricos, & Kleck, 1998; Crawford, 2000; DiIulio, 1991; Kramer & Ulmer, 1996; Miethe & Moore, 1986; Myers & Talarico, 1986; Steffensmeier, Ulmer, & Kramer, 1996; Tonry, 1995; Zatz, 1987; Zimring & Hawkins, 1991; Zimring, Hawkins, & Kamin, 2001).

The Role of Race/Ethnicity in Sentencing Decisions

The influence of extralegal factors on sentencing decisions has revealed somewhat inconclusive findings. Some research shows substantial effects while others show more limited impacts. For example, a number of studies have found a positive relationship between race and sentence severity (Klepper, Nagin, & Tierney, 1983; Petersilia, 1983; Spohn, Delone, & Spears, 1998; Spohn, Gruhl, & Welch, 1981-1982; Steffensmeier & Demuth, 2000; Zatz, 1984), while other studies have reported no significant racial differences (Klein, Petersilia, & Turner, 1990). In fact, some studies have found that Blacks are sentenced more leniently than Whites (Bernstein, Kelly & Doyle, 1977; Gibson, 1978; Levin, 1972).

Some researchers assert that race/ethnic bias in criminal sentencing has declined over time and contend that the predictive power of race/ethnicity, once relevant legal variables are controlled for is quite low (Hagan, 1974; Kleck, 1981; Pruitt & Wilson, 1983; Kramer & Steffensmeier, 1993; Ulmer & Kramer, 1996). Researchers have also argued that race/ethnicity influences sentence severity indirectly through its effect on legal criteria such as bail status (LaFree, 1985; Lizotle, 1978), type of attorney (Spohn, Grugl, & Welch 1981-1982), or type of disposition (LaFree, 1985; Spohn, 1992; Uhlman & Walker, 1980). Some argue that race/ethnicity interacts with both legal and extralegal factors. For example, this interaction affects sentence severity only in some types of cases (Barnett, 1985; Crawford, Chiricos, & Kleck, 1998; Spohn & Cederblom, 1991; Unnever & Hembroff, 1986), in certain settings (Britt, 2000; Hawkins, 1987; Kleck, 1981; Myers & Talarico, 1986), or only for some types of defendants (Chiricos & Bales, 1991; LaFree, 1989; Peterson and Hagan, 1984; Spohn, 1994; Walsh, 1987). The assertion that ethnic minorities are punished more harshly than whites who commit similar crimes is often challenged by those who believe that the harsher sentences which ethnic minorities receive are only a result of their disproportionate involvement in criminal activity.

Exploring the Interaction Between Race/Ethnicity and Legal Criteria: The Liberation Hypothesis

Research has paid close attention to how sentencing outcomes may be a product of the intersection between offense seriousness and race/ethnicity components. According to the liberation hypothesis, the appropriate sentence is determined to a considerable extent by the seriousness of the crime and by the defendant's prior criminal record (Kalven & Zeisel, 1966). Thus, in cases where criminal defendants have committed less serious offenses, courtroom officials vary in their views about appropriate sanctions and allow extralegal variables to play a substantial part in sentencing decisions. Originally, the liberation hypothesis was developed to describe jury behavior (Kalven & Zeisel, 1966). A *liberation process* occurs when jurors consider personal values instead of focusing on legal criteria. The liberation process is most likely to occur in less serious cases because such cases lack direct objective legal criteria to make appropriate sentencing decisions. Kalven and Zeisel (1966) utilized sexual assault cases and distinguish them between aggravated and simple assaults. They found that personal beliefs about the victim's behavior at the time of the incident were more likely to influence the verdict in simple than in aggravated rape cases.

Research has assessed the effect of race/ethnicity on the probability of a prosecutorial request for the death penalty in homicide cases of varying degrees of seriousness. When comparing single and multiple felonies, Paternoster (1984) found that the victim's race/ethnicity was a significant predictor of a death penalty request in cases with one aggravating felony, but this racial influence was significant in multiple felony cases. Other research on the capital sentencing process has revealed similar findings. Barnett (1985) argued that the probability of a death sentence was influenced by the seriousness of the homicide case and found that among homicides in Georgia, the level of seriousness successfully predicted death sentences. When assessing the effects of race/ethnicity of offender, Barnett found that race/ethnicity of the defendant and victim had a significant effect in middle range offenses. Baldus, Woodsworth, and Pulaski (1985) also examined the capital sentencing process in Georgia and found that seriousness index successfully predicted the likelihood of a death sentence. Moreover, they found that the victim's race/ethnicity influenced the decision to sentence the defendant to death, primarily in those cases middle range cases.

Unnever and Hembroff (1987) argue that the influence of a defendant's race/ethnicity depends on the level of uncertainty surrounding the case. By using data on sentenced drug offenders in Miami, Unnever and Hembroff found that the effect of race/ethnicity increased systematically as the case characteristics became increasingly mixed (Unnever and Hembroff, 1987). Spohn and Cederblom (1991) tested the liberation hypothesis with data on the sentencing of felony offenders in Detroit. Spohn and Cederblom found that race/ethnicity had a significant effect on the likelihood of incarceration when the conviction charge was assault as opposed to a more serious felony. Moreover, the effect of race/ethnicity appeared to be restricted primarily to cases where the offender had no prior felony convictions on their record, victimized an acquaintance rather than a stranger, and did not utilize a deadly weapon (Spohn and Cederblom, 1991).

Spohn and Cederblom concluded that judges faced with either criminal offenders convicted of particularly serious crimes or those with substantial records of prior felony convictions had little difficulty deciding whether or not to sentence a defendant to prison. However, the sentencing process of less serious or ambiguous offenses was more difficult and allowed for the influence of extralegal factors.

Not all recent research using the liberation hypothesis to examine disparity in felony sentencing process has produced empirical support for the theory. For example, Keil and Vito (1989) found no support for the liberation hypothesis in the state of Kentucky when they assessed jury decisions in serious felonies and prosecutors' decisions to request the death penalty in capital cases. They found that seriousness of the homicide offense was not a significant predictor in the recommendation of death sentence. They did however find that some racial differentiation was indeed occurring in sentencing outcomes similar to that found in previous studies; Kentucky prosecuting attorneys and jurors alike were most likely to recommend a death sentence for black offenders who killed white victims.

Determinate Sentencing, Sentencing Guidelines, and Rate of Imprisonment

Studies on sentencing reform impacts on the criminal justice system have often reflected a wide range of methodological approaches, thus often producing differing assessments of the true impact of determinate sentences on jail incarceration rates and other important outcomes for criminal justice agencies (D'Alessia & Stolzenberg, 1995; Moody & Marvell, 1996; Stolzenberg & D'Alessia, 1996). It is important to note that sentencing guidelines have been associated with *declines* in prison population growth in six states. In those cases, legislatures required that the framers of sentencing guidelines consider present prison capacity when establishing guidelines for prison sentence lengths (Marvell, 1995).

Unfortunately, the true assessment of sentencing guidelines or determinate sentencing on imprisonment is far from clear. For example, one study reported that Washington's Sentencing Reform Act resulted in convicted offenders either serving shorter prison sentences or in jail facilities rather than in state prison institutions (Elvin, 1989). Consequently, although the official prison population had declined, the number of state inmates under confinement in local jails had increased substantially. What resulted in practice under the Act of 1981 was the effective shortening of sentences for nonviolent offenders and an increase in sentences and time served for serious, violent offenders

The reform of good time credits or the "truth-in-sentencing" phenomenon has reduced the disparity between the sentence prescribed by law and the actual time served by violent offenders in may jurisdictions. Generally, these proposals are designed to require offenders sentenced to prison for violent crimes to serve 85 percent of the imposed sentences. Some have argued that since most truth-in-sentencing proposals were designed to increase time served regardless of the number of prior convictions of offenders, they will have more implications than those of three strikes laws (Austin, 1996). This substantial effect of truth-in-sentencing reforms is attributed to the continual increase of inmates convicted of violent crimes, who serve less than 50 percent of their sentences (Austin, 1996).

California's truth-in-sentencing law restricts good time credits to a maximum of 15 percent for offenders who commit violent crimes (Pestritto, 1995). An even broader statute was proposed in Illinois where all inmates would serve 85 percent of their sentences. The total additional cost to taxpayers in the state of Illinois was estimated to be \$4.6 billion in operating costs and \$1.5 billion in required new construction (Austin, 1996). Results of an analysis on the Illinois truth-in-sentencing proposal indicate that the impact on length of prison stay will vary across offenders. For example, the legislation would significantly increase length of stay for convicted murders, but would extend the sentence of less serious offenders only to a minimal degree (Illinois Truth-in-Sentencing Commission, 1998).

States have taken a variety of other approaches to truth-in-sentencing. Arizona enacted a statute restricting prosecutors from dismissing charges in plea agreements for crimes committed by repeat criminal offenders, in cases of crimes against children, or in those cases where offenders committed a crime while on parole (Hunzeker, 1994). In Tennessee, a law requires the judge in criminal cases to inform the jury of how much time the defendant will serve if convicted of the offenses charged (Hunzeker, 1994). Since 1990, the state of Delaware has had a truth-in-sentencing law which abolished discretionary parole release and limits the ability of the Department of Corrections to release offenders once they have been incarcerated (Quinn, 1992).

In sum, public policy emphasis with respect to sentencing and correctional facilities has shifted from a primarily rehabilitation goal to an established preference for punishment and the systematic incapacitation of offenders through imprisonment. Thus the criminal justice system has resorted to the use of extended periods of incarceration in its effort to reduce future criminal activity. Chronic recidivists, who in fact constitute but a small minority of all offenders, have been responsible for a disproportionately large number of serious crimes (Wolfgang, Figlio, & Sellin, 1972). In an effort to track the lives of criminal offenders, a study examined over 6,000 male offenders who were incarcerated in California prisons in the early 1960s, and over 150,000 male offenders incarcerated during the early 1980s (Gottfredson and Gottfredson, 1993). Data from the 1962 cohort indicated that "nuisance" offenses (i.e., parole and probation violations, gambling, disorderly conduct, drunken driving) followed by property offenses served as the most common subsequent offenses committed by these offenders. Over 30 percent of these offenders were reincarcerated within one year of their release and over half were reincarcerated within three years of release (Gottfredson and Gottfredson, 1993). In reference to their rates of offending, the 1962 cohort experienced an average of .368 arrests per year, and were arrested an average of just over six times. When predicting numbers of rearrests among the 1980 cohort Gottfredson and Gottfredson (1993) found the number of prior periods of incarceration, age, history of opiate use, seriousness of offense, type of commitment, and number of aliases used by the offenders as significantly predicting reoffenses.

While much of the previous research on patterns of crime provide little support for the specialization argument (see Wolfgang, Figlio, & Sellin, 1972; Kempf, 1987; Blumstein, Cohen, & Farrington, 1988), Gottfredson and Gottfredson (1993) did find some support for specialization. Their analysis revealed that the probability of committing a nuisance offense after any type of charge was higher when committing an offense of the same type. When offenders were grouped in terms of the mix of offenses they committed subsequent to release from incarceration, almost 28 percent were committing only nuisance offenses, 17 percent property offenses, 9 percent offenses against persons, and 5 percent fraud (Gottfredson and Gottfredson, 1993).

Selective incapacitation measures like three strikes laws are based on identifying those offenders that present the most risk given their high rate of offending. Unfortunately, it is difficult to classify an offender accurately in terms of the future threat he or she poses to the community. Future dangerousness has often been estimated on the basis of length and seriousness of criminal history record, yet this information alone as a predictive tool has produced rather weak empirical results (Petersilia, 1980; Petersilia, Greenwood, & Lavin, 1978). More recently, studies have shown that crime measure of this sort are not only ineffective (see Auerhahn, 1999) but also have devastating effects on prison populations (Auerhahn, 2002).

The relationship between politics and crime is largely based on American politicians insisting that they are taking steps to reduce serious street crime. With "get tough" reactions, however, they tend to marginalize the social and economic programs that in the long run can prevent criminal behavior. The excessive costs associated with harsh and prolonged punishment comes coming at the expense of crime prevention. Scheingold (1995) has noted that politicians are tough on criminals but not very tough on crime itself. Thus, analyses on the effect of sanctions on future criminality must include assessments on offender characteristics, type of offense, and social settings.

CHAPTER 3

Three Strikes Law and Racial Disparity

The Washington State legislature adopted the Sentencing Reform Act of 1981 that was designed to apply to all felonies committed after June 30, 1984. The Act reformed sentencing process by assuring stiffer punishment and establishing precisely defined sentences to constrain judicial discretion. The Washington State Sentencing Guidelines Commission, an independent agency established by the Act, was directed to create a sentencing structure that would fulfill the above purposes and would "... emphasize confinement for violent offenders and alternatives to total confinement for the nonviolent offender" (Revised Code of Washington 9.94A.040(05)). The commission developed the new sentencing structure over a period of two years, and the state legislature adopted the commission's recommendations in two stages--in 1983 and in 1984.

Sentencing under the new law was to be based on the nature of the criminal act and the offender's criminal history. The sentencing guidelines do allow for departures from the "grid" (i.e., a matrix containing offense and criminal history points with specific ranges of sentences) for "exceptional" sentences, which are either more lenient or more severe than specified in the grid. Judges may depart from the standard sentence in a particular case if there are substantial and compelling reasons for sentences above (aggravated) or below (mitigating) the presumptive term. Such reasons are subject to later judicial review by a higher court. Giving the state legislature control over the specific penalties imposed for particular felonies serve as the most profound change made by the Sentencing Reform Act.

Washington State's Persistent Offender Accountability Act

The State of Washington's initiative process gives voters direct power to enact new laws by petitioning to place proposed legislature on a statewide general election ballot. To certify an issue to the ballot, the initiative's sponsor must circulate the complete text of the proposal among voters and obtain voter signatures equaling eight percent of the number of votes cast for the office of Governor at the last regular gubernatorial election. Once on the ballot, the initiative becomes law upon receiving a majority of voter approval.

Initiative 593 or the three strikes law, declared that community protection from persistent offenders was a high priority concern for any civilized society. Moreover, it also indicated that nearly 50 percent of the criminal offenders convicted in the state of Washington have active prior criminal histories. The initiative called for punishments proportionate to both the seriousness of the crime and the prior criminal history of the offender. Lastly, the public referendum noted that citizens had the constitutional right and civic responsibility to determine when to impose a life sentence for repeat violent offenders.[2] The fact that Washington voters assumed that such a law was necessary is not surprising. The views of Washington citizens on crime and crime policy mirror those held by the citizens nationwide. In general, the public believes that the criminal justice system does not deal harshly enough with offenders.

After the passage of the law in Washington State some efforts were made to repeal the statute. The Washington Association of Criminal Defense Lawyers created a "Three Strikes Task Force" which began briefing a variety of challenges to the legality of the initiative in Washington's very liberal constitutional setting. Such efforts failed and constitutional challenges to the Washington law continue to be unsuccessful. Interestingly, Initiative 593 is not Washington's only law aimed at habitual recidivists. Washington also has a "habitual criminal" (Revised Code of Washington 9.92.090). When comparing the three strikes law to the habitual criminal statue, the two are quite similar. They both apply upon the third conviction for a certain specific offense and both define status on the basis of at least two prior convictions for certain types of serious

---

[2] In 1992, a similar measure to Initiative 593 failed to get the signatures needed for ballot certification. Some have argued that the 1993 initiative's support received from the National Rifle Association made its passage and support difficult (National Public Radio Broadcast, October 14, 1993).

crimes. Also, each applies a penalty of life imprisonment to the most recent conviction. The only substantive difference lies in the types of offenses included in the statutes.

While scholars continue to attempt to forecast the impact of three strikes laws in large states such as Texas and California (Austin et al, 1999; Caulkins, 2001; Marvel & Moody, 2001; Meehan, 2001; Wright, 1995), studies on the development of sentencing reform indicate increasing support for the implementation of such laws (Applegate, Cullen, Turner, & Sundt, 1996). Interestingly, some research has argued for the repeal of all mandatory minimum penalties, including three strikes laws (Tonry, 1996; Greenwood et al., 1996; Cushman, 1996; Austin, 1996).

Between 1993 and 1995, 24 states and the federal government enacted new laws employing the three strikes label[3] (Clark, Austin, & Henry, 1997, 1998). Except for Kansas, all of the states that enacted three strikes laws had pre-existing statutes that targeted repeat violent offenders. While the legal definition of a *strike* varies considerably from state to state, violent felonies such as homicide, rape, assault, and arson are included in virtually all three strikes provisions. Differences exist in the number of strikes needed for offenders to be sentenced to a life term. For example, in Montana and Georgia offenders must only commit two strikable offenses yet, the majority of states,

---

[3] States with three strikes laws include: Arkansas, California, Colorado, Connecticut, Florida, Georgia, Indiana, Kansas, Louisiana, Maryland, Montana, Nevada, New Jersey, New Mexico, North Carolina, North Dakota, Pennsylvania, South Carolina, Tennessee, Utah, Vermont, Virginia, Washington, and Wisconsin (Clark, Austin, & Henry, 1997, 1998).

offenders must commit three strikes (Clark, Austin, & Henry, 1997).

The type of punishment imposed when offenders reach the sufficient number of strikes also varies. A sanction of mandatory life imprisonment without the possibility of parole is the sentence given to offenders within the states of Georgia, Indiana, Louisiana, Maryland, Montana, New Jersey, North Carolina, South Carolina, Tenseness, Virginia, Washington, and Wisconsin (Clark, Austin, & Henry, 1997). The states of New Mexico, Colorado, and California allow for the provision of parole once a minimum of 25 years have been served.

Interestingly, when first proposed in the state of Washington, determinate sentencing received rather severe criticism from state court judges and the state's parole board. Critics of sentencing reform expressed fear in prison overcrowding and an indiscriminate increase in sentence lengths (Shane-Du-Bow, Brown, & Olsen, 1985). Sentencing figures and forecasts released from the Washington State Department of Corrections and the Washington State Sentencing Guidelines Commission state that the mandatory life sentences provision of the three strikes initiative will cause the state's prison population to increase by 400 inmates by the year 2006 (Miller, August 14, 1994).

Currently, there are 199 third strike offenders in the state of Washington serving life without the possibility of parole (Statistical Summary of Adult Felony Sentencing Fiscal Year 2001, 2002). While the state's correctional facility population is over 13,000 inmates, the fiscal impact of third strike offenders will increase over time as offenders age and their medical care needs increase and as the number of third strike convictions increases (The

Olympian, November 10, 1997). The problems with the aging prison population have already been documented in the state of California (see Auerhahn, 2002).

Glass (1997) has identified some of the more obvious flaws in the logic of three strikes laws and noted that the Justice Department advertised the law as a success while growing research showed that the impact of selective incapacitation was less than effective. For example, Gottfredson and Gottfredson (1993) indicate the following:

> Proposals for dramatic change in sentencing and incarceration policies based on individual level prediction studies are at best premature. Predictions of such low validity as thus far demonstrated cannot justify the policy changes proposed under the banner of selective incapacitation (Gottfredson and Gottfredson, 1993: 10).

Research will continue to track in detail the impact of three strikes laws on each stage of the criminal justice system (i.e., bail setting, detention, time to trial, type of trial, plea negotiations, and jail and prison population levels). Criminal justice officials and practitioners often exercise their considerable discretion to avoid the application of laws they consider unduly harsh. Arrest rates for target crimes typically decline soon after mandatory sentencing laws take effect. Also, dismissal and diversion rates tend to increase at early stages of case processing after mandatory sentencing laws take effect. Are Washington State's criminal justice system actors also making such discretionary choices in the application of mandatory sentencing laws? Are they using their professional discretion in a racially and ethically neutral manner, or is there evidence of disparate effects upon minority groups? These are the types of public policy concerns that need to receive careful attention in Washington State and across the country.

Research Questions

In order to examine the extent to which racial/ethnic and legal criteria influence the sentencing process of repeat and third strike offenders, the following research questions will be tested. Hypotheses 1a - 1h concern the relationship between race/ethnicity and sentence length for repeat offenders. It is argued that minority offenders-- including Blacks, Asians, Native Americans, and Hispanics--will in general receive longer sentences than White offenders (Research Question 1a.). This research question is consistent with findings on racial/ethnic impact and sentence length (Spohn, Gruhl, & Welch, 1981-1982; Spohn & Cederblom, 1991). In order to examine the different racial/ethnic impact on the sentencing of various types of offenses, several research questions will be tested. Research Question 1b. assess the sentencing of racial/ethnic minorities in more serious cases and Research Question 1c. examines the sentencing of racial/ethnic minorities in less serious cases.

<u>Research Question 1a</u>. Will minority offenders receive lengthier total sentences than White offenders?

<u>Research Question 1b</u>. Will race/ethnicity have a significant effect on the sentencing of murder, robbery, and firearm cases?

Research Question 1c. Will race/ethnicity have a significant effect on the sentencing of assault, theft, drug, and residential burglary cases?

Previous research has attempted to explore unwarranted sentence disparity under sentencing guidelines. For example, Moore and Miethe (1986) found that black defendants in Minnesota were less likely to receive departures below sentencing guidelines. Griswold (1987) found that level of offenses seriousness and prior criminal record were the main predictors in sentencing departures. Kramer and Steffensmeier (1993) found significant race and gender differences in incarceration decisions (i.e., prison/jail vs. probation). However, they found that race differences in incarceration decreased when sentences that departed below the guidelines were removed from the model. In order to further explore racial/ethnic bias among minority repeat and third strike offenders, sentencing guideline departures will serve as a measure of sentence severity. By utilizing three ratio variables previously used in the literature assessing sentence disparity (see Griswold, 1987; Kramer & Ulmer, 1996), the assumption will be made that while minority offenders are more likely to have departures above guidelines (Research Question 2a.), race/ethnicity will not have an effect on overall sentence departure and below sentence departure (Hypotheses 2b. and 2c.).

Research Question 2a. Will race/ethnicity have a significant effect on above guideline departure for both strike and non-strike offense cases?

<u>Research Question 2b</u>. Will race/ethnicity have a significant effect on overall guideline departures?

<u>Research Question 2c</u>. Will race/ethnicity have a significant effect on below guidelines departure for both strike and non-strike offense cases?

The likelihood of utilizing plea bargaining as a means of obtaining a less severe sentence has also been previously examined in the sentencing literature. Research indicates that trial defendants were more likely to be sentenced to prison and those that were incarcerated received an average of 13.55 more months on their sentence than defendants who plea bargained their cases (Walsh, 1990). Spohn and Cederblom (1991) found that defendants who had a jury trial were more likely than other defendants to be sent to prison, and their expected minimum sentence was nearly three years longer. It is hypothesized that minority offenders are less likely to use this tool while being more likely to receive a community supervision sentence once released from confinement.

<u>Research Question 3</u>. Will race/ethnicity have a significant effect on decisions to Plea Bargain?

<u>Research Question 4</u>. Will race/ethnicity will have a significant effect on decisions to allocate Community Supervision?

In order to identify the presence of racial/ethnic bias among criminal offenders who commit specific offenses, it is necessary to carefully match cases in such comparisons and go beyond simple aggregate comparison across racial/ethnic categories of offenders. When identifying and incarcerating serious chronic offenders, attention is in fact given to the level of seriousness of offenders' criminal histories. In order to fully explore the effect of patterns of previous offenses on future criminality, research must also consider the various types of offenses, which repeat offenders choose to commit. For the purpose of this study, repeat offenders consist of those offenders who have been convicted of at least one strike and any other felony offense during the period 1992 to 1997. Three strike offenders consist of offenders who have been incarcerated for life for committing three most serious offenses since the enactment of the law.

Research Question 5. Will repeat and three strike offenders who have been convicted of a property offense have a higher probability of committing a subsequent property offense?

Research Question 6. Will repeat and three strike offenders who have been convicted of a violent personal offense have a lower probability of committing a subsequent violent personal offense?

Research Question 7. Will repeat offenders who have been convicted of a drug offenses have a higher probability of committing a subsequent property offense?

Research Question 8. Will repeat and three strike offenders who have been convicted of a sex offense have a lower probability of committing a subsequent sex offense.

CHAPTER 4

Methodology

In this chapter, I present the methodology used in this study. This study relies on both quantitative and qualitative data in order to assess the possible presence of racial/ethnic disparity in the sentencing of repeat offenders (including three strike offenders) who commit less serious offenses, the tracking of offense patterns of repeat offenders who have committed serious violent offenses, and the character of perceptions held by public officials who process these offenders in counties with high proportions of experience with the three strike offenders within the state of Washington.

The objectives of this aspect of this study are trifold. A primary objective of this study is to provide a more comprehensive test of the liberation hypothesis by examining the effect of race/ethnicity on a series of case processing decisions comparing outcomes for ethnic minorities and for white offenders charged with a variety of similar felony offenses. While previous studies have focused on the sentencing decision, the data set used in this study includes information on conviction and sentencing decisions for offenders charged with serious violent offenses. Among these offenses are violence against persons, property crimes, sex crimes, and record of drug offenses. The data will be used to test the research question that racial/ethnic bias in case processing decisions is confined to less serious cases, where circumstances surrounding the offense are unclear and less certain.

The second major objective is to assess the pattern of offenses in order to predict the odds of committing subsequent offenses. This will be accomplished by exploring patterns within sequences of criminal activity. Effort will be devoted to the development of an event sequence for those felony criminal offenders in the state of Washington who have been sentenced for committing one, two or three *most serious offenses*. Because the legislative intent underlying the three strikes law in the state of Washington is to incarcerate offenders convicted of multiple (three) felonies, the criminal history of these offenders becomes pivotal in conviction and sentencing decisions.

The literature on sentencing outcomes, while often attempting to capture the decision making process of courtroom personnel, often lacks the in-depth personal perception of court personnel who are responsible for the processing of offenders. In order to obtain such information, interview data from public officials who process the majority of violent offender cases will be utilized. This method allows these officials to comment on their perception of the enactment of the three strikes law and how it has affected their courtroom environment.

Assessing the Impact of Race/Ethnicity on Sentence Type and Length of Incarceration

The data for this assessment were obtained from the State of Washington Sentencing Guidelines Commission, whose staff provided data sets for the fiscal years 1993 - 1997. The Commission has collected and recorded data on all felony convictions within the state since 1987. In order to assess the possible occurrence of racial/ethnic disparity in the sentencing of chronic offenders, data were obtained on convictions which involved either the sentencing of a third strike case or the sentencing of a non-strike felony committed by offenders who had at least one strike in his/her criminal history record. This data set contained information on criminal offender characteristics, type of felony conviction(s), and type and length of sentence imposed on the offender.

According to the State of Washington Sentencing Guidelines Commission Annual Report (1997), Washington State averages 19,000 felony convictions per year. Among these convictions, approximately 3,700 are felony convictions which involve the processing of a third strike offense or a non-strike offense committed by an offender who has at least one strike in their criminal history record. A total of 19,403 convictions involving the previously noted offenses were obtained from the Commission for the fiscal years 1993 - 1997. It should once again be noted that this includes the records of all offenders in the state who have at least one strike in their criminal history record. One could refer to this as a sample of time, since it includes the convictions of all offenders who have been formally affected by this law since the passage of the law.

Selection bias within this population can be identified as a problem in as much as offenders who may have been discriminated in earlier processes of the system (e.g., arrest and charging) are not included in this population. The data utilized in this study contains all offenders processed under the Washington law. This chronic offender population has been identified by statute and court decisions as being the most dangerous societal subgroup, and most in need of a long period of incarceration to insure public safety. For the first analytical technique, the unit of analysis is sentences of repeat offenders who have at least one strike in their criminal history record. Since the sentence is the unit of analysis, offenders may appear in the data set multiple times.

The data used for these analyses include only cases sentenced within the state of Washington. Every county is responsible for submitting a judgment and sentence form to the State of Washington Sentencing Guidelines Commission for offenders who have been sentenced for a felony within their respective counties. The acquisition of cases where offenders were not sentenced was beyond the scope of this study due to the primary interest in assessing possible disparity in the treatment of minorities among this specialized population of criminal defendants--namely repeat offenders. However, the potential for selection bias should be recognized and noted.

The data from the Sentencing Guidelines Commission was utilized for two main reasons. First, the data contained not only sentences of felony convictions over the past five years, but also allowed for an assessment of racial/ethnic impact on sentences because it contains information on four identifiable ethnic groups. These racial/ethnic groups include Blacks, Asians, Native Americans, and Hispanics. Second, the data collected by the State of Washington Sentencing Guidelines Commission contain not a sample of cases but rather a population of all offenders who have been sentenced for strike offenses. While the three strikes law in the state of Washington was enacted in December 1993, the law is applied retroactively. For example, offenders who were sentenced prior to the enactment of the law for an offense(s) that is equivalent to a strikable offense will automatically have a strike(s) in their criminal history record.

Measurement

In order to examine the possible presence of racial/ethnic bias in the treatment of offenders convicted of less serious offenses, three primary assessments are taken. The first analysis predicts the effect of race/ethnicity on the total sentence length received for either a strike offense or a non-strike offense. In order to further explore the research question that racial/ethnic bias is restricted to less serious cases, separate multivariate regression models for each type of case were run. This analysis included models predicting sentence length for Murder,[4] Robbery, Firearm-related offense, Assault, Theft, Drug, and Residential Burglary cases. The second set of models attempts to capture any sentence guideline disparity occurring among repeat offenders. Models assessing overall guidelines departure judgment both below guidelines and above guidelines were run to capture any evidence of disparate racial/ethnic

---

[4] Murder and Manslaughter offenses were combined for this analysis.

impact on the use of exceptional sentences. The same guidelines departure ratios used in recent literature to address the sentence disparity question are utilized in this analysis (Griswold, 1987; Kramer & Ulmer, 1996). The third series of regression models will estimate the influence of race/ethnicity on cases resulting in guilty pleas and on the decision to have certain offenders serve community supervision once released from confinement. The measurement of these variables will allow for the assessment of sentencing outcomes differences while controlling for all relevant variables (i.e., offender characteristics, case seriousness, and case characteristics).

A subgroup of offenders included in the data set have received *specialized* sentences for their offenses. For example, sex offenders may have received a suspended sentence that may include a jail term of up to six months and required outpatient or inpatient treatment. Since these offenders have received below guideline departures which are attributed to the Special Sex Offender Sentencing Alternative (SSOSA) law in the state rather than as a consequence of judicial discretion, these sentences have been removed from the analyses. Also, first-time offenders may receive a first offense waiver (FTOW) which allows the court broad discretion in setting a sentence. These cases have also been removed from the analysis since statutory rather than judicial discretion determined length of sentence. The general model for this analysis is as follows:

$$Y_i = a + b_1x_{i1} + b_2x_{i2} + b_3x_{i3} + b_4x_{i4} + b_5x_{i5} + b_6x_{i6} + b_7x_{i7} + b_8x_{i8} + b_9x_{i9} + b_{10}x_{i10} + b_{11}x_{i11} + b_{12}x_{i12} + b_{13}x_{i13} + b_{14}x_{i14} + b_{15}x_{i15} + b_{16}x_{i16} + b_{17}x_{i17} + b_{18}x_{i18} + b_{19}x_{i19} + b_{20}x_{i20} + b_{21}x_{i21} + b_{22}x_{i22} + b_{23}x_{i23} + b_{24}x_{i24}$$

where y_i refers to the total sentence in months for the ith sentence

x_{i1} = age of offender in the ith sentence
x_{i2} = sex of offender in the ith sentence
x_{i3} = offender is Black in the ith sentence
x_{i4} = offender is Asian in the ith sentence
x_{i5} = offender is Native American in the ith sentence
x_{i6} = offender is Hispanic in the ith sentence
x_{i7} = time offender convicted in the ith sentence
x_{i8} = counts of offender in i^{th} sentence
x_{i9} = offender committed Murder 1 or 2 in the ith sentence
x_{i10} = offender committed Manslaughter in the ith sentence
x_{i11} = offender committed Robbery in the ith sentence
x_{i12} = offender committed Assault 1 or 2 in the ith sentence
x_{i13} = offender committed Burglary in the ith sentence
x_{i14} = offender committed Rape 1, 2 or 3 in the ith sentence
x_{i15} = offender committed Other Sex Offense in the ith sentence
x_{i16} = offender committed Kidnapping in the ith sentence
x_{i17} = offender committed Vehicular Homicide in the ith sentence
x_{i18} = offender committed Other Strike Offense in i^{th} sentence
x_{i19} = offender received weapon enhancement in the ith sentence
x_{i20} = level of seriousness of offender in the ith sentence
x_{i21} = prior number of offenses for offender in the ith sentence
x_{i22} = prior number of strikes for offender in the ith sentence
x_{i23} = guilty plea for offender in the ith sentence
x_{i24} = jury trial for offender in the ith sentence

The operationalization of these variables is discussed in the following section.

Dependent Variables

In order to examine the effect of race/ethnicity on sentencing decisions, a total of 13 dependent variables are included in this analytical section. The dependent variables include Total Sentence Received, Murder Sentence Received, Robbery Sentence Received, Firearm Sentence Received, Assault Sentence Received, Theft Sentence Received, Drug Sentence Received, and Residential Burglary Sentence Received, all of which are measured in months. In order to measure the amount by which sentences deviate or depart from guidelines, three ratios were utilized. Griswold's (1987) measure of all guideline departures includes the midpoint of guideline ranges as a baseline.[5] This dependent variable will be referred to as the Overall Sentence Departure. Thus, the ratio captures all departures, overall, above and below guideline provisions. In order to further examine whether race/ethnicity has an influence on sentence disparity for repeat offenders, two other ratios will be utilized. Kramer and Ulmer (1996) have created the measures of below and above guidelines departures. *Below Guidelines Departure* is calculated by selecting only those cases where a below guidelines departure is possible and cases where a received sentence was below the minimum guidelines range for that type of offense. Once these cases are identified, the ratio measures

[5] Griswold's (1987) ratio is calculated: (guideline range midpoint-actual received sentence)/ guideline range midpoint. This ratio ranges from -1 to 22 months (see also Table 1 for descriptive statistics).

the proportion of the guideline minimum sentence by which the received minimum sentence falls below the guideline minimum.[6] In order to measure Above Guideline Departure, the selection of those cases where an above guideline departure existed were identified for analysis. A ratio was then created which measured the proportion of the guideline maximum sentence by which the received sentence falls above the guideline maximum.[7] In order to examine whether race/ethnicity has an influence on the decision to hand down a Community Supervision Sentence, logistic regression models are used to assess the odds of receiving this post-incarceration sanction as well (Community Supervision = 1; No Community Supervision = 0).

The impact of mode of disposition has revealed interesting results in previous literature. For example, Walsh (1990) found that cases that go to trial tend to be those involving serious crimes against a person (such as murder or rape). The cases least likely to go to trial were sexual molestation due to the lack of willingness of prosecutors to place children on the stand and force them to testify. The model assessing modes of dispositions will take these findings into account and assess those cases least likely to result in plea bargaining.

Mode of disposition becomes important in this assessment because of the leverage that prosecutors posses when they are able to plea bargain a case. For example,

---

[6] Below guidelines departures is calculated: (guideline minimum sentence - received minimum sentence)/ guideline minimum sentence. This ratio ranges from 0 to 1 (Kramer & Ulmer, 1996).

[7] Above guidelines departures is calculated:
(received maximum sentence - guideline maximum sentence)/ guideline maximum sentence. This ratio ranges from .0025 to 14.

certain offenders may be offered the opportunity to plead down to a lesser degree offense which may not qualify as a third strike offense. Thus, are repeat and third strike offenders more likely to plea bargain their cases or elect a jury or bench trial? In order to examine the mode of disposition among this chronic offender population, the final dependent variable in this section is *Guilty Plea* (Yes = 1; No = 0) which will be predicted with logistic regression.

Independent Variables

The independent variables include several measures variables of specific interest and various control variables. Offense is divided into 11 categories- Murder, Manslaughter, Robbery 1 or 2, Assault 1 or 2, Burglary, Rape 1,2, or 3, Other Sex Offense,[8] Kidnapping, Vehicular Homicide, Other Strike Offense,[9] and Any Other Felony Offense. Dummy variable categories were created for each of the variables except for Any Other Felony Offense, which is the reference category. *Race/ethnicity* is coded into five dummy variable categories: White, Black, Asian, Hispanic, and Native American, with White serving as the reference category. All models include a control for sex of the offender (Male = 1; Female = 0), *Age* (which refers to

---

[8] Other Sex Offense includes: Rape of Child; Child Molestation; Incest; Indecent Liberties; and Sexual Exploitation.

[9] Other Strike Offense includes: Homicide by Abuse; Controlled Substance Homicide; Bail Jumping with Murder 1; Assault of Child 1 and 2; Vehicular Assault; Arson; Leading Organized Crime; Extortion 1; Promoting Prostitution; Damaging Building by Explosion with Threat to Human Being; Endangering Life and Property by Explosives with Threat to Human Being; Explosive Devises Prohibited; Possession of Incendiary Device; Malicious Injury to Railroad Property.

the age of the defendant at the time of conviction), Guilty Plea (Yes = 1; No = 0), and Jury Trial (Yes = 1; No = 0). Since offenders may receive a sentence enhancement for use of a weapon during a felony offense, the need for control for such enhancements is also taken into account. While sentencing research has identified the importance of prior record when predicting sentence severity, there is little consensus among researchers regarding the appropriate measure for the operationalization of prior record. Legal research has utilized arrest record, convictions, incarceration and a combination of all three to classify offenders as to the length and seriousness of prior criminal history record. Moreover, the advisability of using exclusively felony or a combination of felony and misdemeanor arrests or convictions is often unclear. Caution should be taken when utilizing these measures of prior record interchangeably due to the different effects they may have on White and minority criminal offenders. It has been shown that the use of certain measures of criminal history record result in specific research outcomes. For example, prior felony convictions and prior incarcerations are significantly associated with sentence severity (Welch, Gruhl, & Spohn, 1984). However, it has been shown that neither previous arrest nor previous felony arrests are significantly associated with sentence severity. Also, measures of conviction are highly correlated and can be used interchangeably to assess sentence severity.

According to Welch et al. (1984), prior incarceration has the most uniform effect on the sentence of both white and minority defendants. The data for this study include the following measures of prior record: prior number of strike offenses, prior number of non-strike offenses, whether or not defendant has ever been sentenced to prison for longer than a year for a strike felony conviction, and number of times a defendant has been sentenced to prison for longer than a year for a strike felony conviction.

The data used for this study contain repeat offenders who have committed a strike felony offense and offenders who have been convicted of a non-strike felony offense, but have a documented strike offense in their criminal history record. The argument could be made that all offenses committed by this population comprise serious offenses since they are *all felonies*. However, one must take into account the fact that not all cases are equally serious. In fact, one of that major controversies surrounding three strikes law is the notion that the law includes offenses which are not properly regarded as serious; certain unquestionable offenses (e.g., first degree murder, first degree rape, felonies committed with a weapon) do exist and can be distinguished from the more questionable offenses.

In order to distinguish between more and less serious cases, the following indicators were used: most serious conviction charge (Murder 1 and 2, Manslaughter, Robbery 1 and 2, Assault 1 and 2, Burglary, Rape, Other Sex Offenses, Kidnapping, Vehicular Homicide, Firearm Related Offense, Assault 3, Residential Burglary, Theft, Taking a Motor Vehicle Without Owner's Permission, Possession of Stolen Property, Forgery, and Drug Offense); number of prior felony offenses (ranging 0 to 10); number of prior strike offenses (ranging from 1 to 3); level of offense seriousness (ranging from 0 to 15); and use of weapon in commission of offense. In order to control for exogenous legal variables Sentenced Date (ranging July 1992 through June 1997) and Number of Counts (ranging from 0 to 10), were also included in the analyses.

Tables 1 - 4 contain the descriptive statistics for all variables, while Appendix A sets forth the correlations among all variables. Table 1 reveals that the average age of offenders sentenced within the data is 30 years. Sentenced offenders average approximately 1.3 counts and 1.5 prior offenses. The average length of sentence for offenders is 2 _ years. As Table 2 indicates, 65 percent (N = 11,980) of the defendants were White, while 24 percent (N = 4,534) of the defendants are Black. Hispanic defendants constitute 6 percent (N = 1,100) of the population and Asian and Native American defendants comprise the remaining 5 percent of offenders within the data. As shown in Table 3, Male defendants make-up 94 percent of the data. Approximately 90 percent (N = 17,380) of the cases processed under the law have resulted in plea bargaining and 9 percent (N= 1,699) resulted in jury trials. A weapon was involved in 6 percent (N= 1,150) of the cases, while 23 percent (N = 4,270) of cases resulted in a community supervision sentence. Table 4 indicates that 13 percent of the defendants received a below guidelines sentence and 4 percent received an above guidelines sentence.

Analyzing Sentencing Decisions

In order to estimate the impact of Race/ethnicity on the various sentence types and lengths, regression equations were constructed. By utilizing Ordinary Least Squares regression, a multivariate analysis for the total sentence received is computed. Furthermore, in order to test whether racial/ethnic bias in the sentencing of repeat offenders is confined to less serious cases, separate multivariate analyses for each type of case were performed. OLS regression models were also computed to estimate the impact of race/ethnicity and legal variables on guideline departures. Logistic regression models were constructed to examine the two dichotomous dependent variables: guilty plea and community supervision. These models include all relevant control variables, including those for strike and non-strike offenses.

Event Sequence Analysis

The ability to identify a pattern of offenses committed by repeat offenders allows for the test of the question-–what are the proportion of specialists and generalists among such an offender population. The repeat offender population in this study contained the most chronic offenders in the state (three strike offenders), thus allowing for the assessment of their criminal history records. This analytical technique entailed examining the pattern of offenses for offenders who have at least one strike in their criminal history record and offenders sentenced for at least three strike offenses.[10] Thus, a distinction is made between those offenders who have been incarcerated for life under the three strikes law and those offenders who have been convicted of at least one strike offense.

The data for this examination was also obtained from the State of Washington Sentencing Guidelines Commission. Fiscal year data from 1993 - 1997 contains felony convictions of offenders who have at least one strike in their criminal history record. Offenders were matched within the five-year data set in order to obtain the most

---

[10] There were offenders who had more than three strike offenses. For example, offenders who had committed only non-strike offenses since the enactment of the law but have more than three strikes in their criminal history record.

recent and accurate description of the sentencing records of repeat offenders in the state. A total of 2,581 offenders were identified as having at least one strike conviction.[11] The offenders serving life imprisonment constituted a separate data set (N = 105).[12] Thus, three strike offenders and offenders with at least one strike convictions serve as the two samples of interest.

In order to analyze the sequential pattern of offenses committed by repeat offenders in the state of Washington, categories of offenses (events) were constructed for each offender. These events were entered in the order of time they occurred. Thus, offense committed at T1 was followed by an offense committed at T2. In order to test whether repeat and third strike offenders commit similar or different subsequent crimes, contingency tables for both types of offenders were created. Offenses committed by repeat offenders were categorized into 18 offense types. These categories include: Murder,[13] Robbery 1 and 2, Burglary, Assault 1 and 2, Rape 1, 2, and 3, Other Sex Offense, Kidnapping, Vehicular Homicide, Firearm, Assault 3, Residential Burglary, Theft 1 and 2, Taking a Motor Vehicle Without Owners Permission, Possession of Stolen Property, Forgery, Drug Offenses, Other Strike Offense, and Other Felony. Due to the lower variability of offenses committed by three strike offenders, only 10 categories of offenses were created for this particular

---

[11] Cases containing offenders sentenced more than twice were dropped from the analysis of repeat offenders because of the small number of cases.

[12] While there are currently 100 third strike offenders in the state of Washington, data was made available for only 105 of those offenders.

Murder includes Murder 1 and 2, Manslaughter, and Aggravated Murder.

sample. These categories include Murder, Kidnapping, Assault, Robbery, Burglary, Arson, Rape, Prostitution, Indecent Liberties, and Child Molestation. Separate probabilities are obtained for White male, White female, Black male, Black female and Hispanic offenders. Due to the small number of cases, probabilities for Native American and Asian offenders are not presented. The primary focus of this analytical section is to determine whether these offenders committed the same offenses during their crime span or select various types of criminal offenses.

Statistical Technique

By utilizing Bakeman and Quera's (1995) Sequential Data Interchange Standard (SDIS) program and Generalized Sequential Querier (GSEQ), contingency tables were created for both repeat offenders and for the third strike offenders who have been incarcerated for life under the three strikes law. These programs are designed to specifically analyze sequential data. In order to examine the sequence of offenses committed by offenders, conditional probabilities and adjusted residuals (*z* scores) were obtained. For example, the probability of committing a Murder at T1 and T2 is presented. In order to examine whether offenders of different race/ethnicity commit different sequence of offenses, conditional probabilities are presented for Whites, Blacks, Asians, Native American and Hispanics. Gender differences are also explored. Due to the small number of women and racial/ethnic minorities among the three strike sample, women were dropped from the analyses and only conditional probabilities for White and minority offenders are examined.

Elite Interviews

In order to assess the impact of the three strikes law on the judicial system in the state of Washington, telephone interviews were arranged with public officials within the state of Washington. Public officials who are responsible for processing the cases of violent offenders in their respective counties serve as the targeted sample. Public officials in this study included prosecuting attorneys and defense attorneys. In order to obtain accurate information on the processing of such offenders, contact was made with prosecutors and defense attorneys within the state.

A sample of convenience was originally planned as the sampling method. King, Pierce, and Snohomish counties were selected due to the large number of felony convictions arising from these counties each year. According to the State of Washington Sentencing Guidelines Commission (1997), approximately 68 percent of all third strike offenders were convicted in these three counties. However, once contact was made with two of the three prosecutors offices, it was revealed that only two deputy prosecuting attorneys handle the processing of third strike offenders in those two counties. In order to increase the sample size, every prosecutors and assigned counsel office in the state was contacted. After explaining the purpose underlying this study, contacts within the counties referred the researcher to officials who have the most familiarity with the processing of third strike offenders. Contact with other attorneys in the county was made possible through the snowball sampling technique.

The purpose of these interviews was three-fold. First, in order to capture an understanding of the impact of the three strikes law on these offices, information on the procedures taken when processing felony offenders was needed. Therefore, it was essential that the public officials within these offices presented their inner workings or work culture. Second, the public officials who process these cases would be responsible for the implementation of the law and would provide the impact experienced by criminal justice agencies, whether fiscally, administratively and/or politically. Lastly, the prosecution of an offender who potentially faces a life sentence is very different in terms of severity from the sentencing of other violent offenders. Thus, such information would be provided by the public officials.

Several precautions were taken in order to secure insightful responses. Due to the busy schedules of attorneys, interviews lasted between ten and twelve minutes. However, efforts were made during certain interviews (which lasted approximately 30 minutes) to allow respondents to follow-up on any question and expand on any question or comment if he or she desired. In an effort to avoid any misunderstanding of technical language, efforts were made to become familiar with legal terminology, including offense codes and knowledge on the new sentence enhancements passed within the past six years. This was done in order to interpret, comprehend, evaluate, or respond to statements made by respondents. Moreover, efforts were made to probe when any ambiguous or unclear responses were stated by the attorneys.

As suggested by Gorden (1992), responses by the attorneys were evaluated in context. Thus, responses were related to the specific counties where these public officials processed violent offender cases. In order to evaluate responses, several precautions were taken before drawing conclusions. First, it was determined whether the respondent was actually answering the specific question(s) or expanding on a comment. Second, determination was made on whether the answers were complete. Precautions were taken for responses that may have been relevant but were not complete. The degree of relevance of responses was also assessed. For example, emphasis was given to only felony cases. Thus specific attention was devoted to the relevancy of the objective, person, situation, time period, or event referred to in the response.

There were several procedures that were taken into account when recording the attorneys' responses. These included precoding structured answers, writing notes from memory after the completion of each interview, taking minimal notes during the interview and amplifying once completion of interview was reached, and taking verbatim notes during the interview (Maxfield & Babbie, 1998). Lastly, as recommended by Fowler (1993) and Gorden (1992) coding categories were created to classify responses from prosecuting attorneys based on the interview questions.

CHAPTER 5

Analytical Results

The following chapter presents the results of the three analytical techniques. In order to explore the sentencing decisions of repeat offenders, specifically three strike offenders, differing modes of analyses are used to explore whether racial/ethnic disparity exists in a sentencing guidelines context. First, results from the test of the liberation hypothesis are presented. Then, results from an examination of patterned offenses are discussed. Finally, the chapter concludes with a presentation of various qualitative statements derived from public officials within the state.

Testing the Liberation Hypothesis

Findings from Research Question 1a: Will minority offenders receive lengthier total sentences than White offenders?

Assessments of the influence of race/ethnicity on total sentence reveals that an offender's race/ethnicity significantly predicts the total sentence received. However, this applies only for Asian offenders (Table 5). While Asian offenders receive five months more than White offenders, this provides little support for racial/ethnic bias in sentencing. When examining specific offenses, the felonies of Murder, Assault and Rape have a positive effect on total sentence length. While Murder and Rape are regarded a serious offenses (Spohn & Cederblom, 1991), it is interesting to note that Assault, classified as a less serious offense, has a positive effect on total sentence as well. Manslaughter, Robbery, Burglary, other Sex Offenses and Vehicular Homicide have a negative effect on total sentence. A weapon enhancement sentence increases sentence length by 22 months for all offenders. Legal variables such as level of seriousness of offense, prior number of offenses, and prior number of strikes all have a positive effect on sentence length; these findings are consistent with those of Griswold (1987). As expected, cases which result in a Guilty plea have a negative effect on sentence length, while Jury trial cases have a positive effect. Guilty plea cases receive 8 months less than those offenders who choose a Bench trial (reference category), while Jury trial cases receive an additional 18 months longer sentence than a Bench trial case.

Based on these assessments of race/ethnicity on total sentence received, one can conclude that the results provide minimal support for the argument that racial/ethnic disparity exists when sentencing minority offenders. The positive effect of Assault cases (a less serious offense) on sentence length may be attributed to stiffer penalties since becoming a strike offense. It is clear that legally based offender characteristics are significant predictors of sentence length and not racial/ethnic variables. Results on mode of disposition provide support for the argument that offenders who choose a Jury trial are penalized by receiving longer sentences than offenders who choose a Bench trial.

Findings from Research Question 1b: Will race/ethnicity have a significant effect on the sentencing of murder, robbery, and firearm related cases?

The liberation hypothesis is based on the notion that race/ethnicity becomes important only in the sentencing of less serious crimes. Consistent with this research question, results in Table 6 indicate that when predicting total sentence for Murder cases, race/ethnicity is insignificant. This may be attributed to the possible clear-cut heinous nature of the offense. In such cases, extra legal variables such as race/ethnicity become insignificant. Level of seriousness of offense, number of prior offenses and strikes all show a statistically significant effect on the sentencing of these cases. Guilty plea and Jury trials did not have a significant effect in the sentencing of these cases. It is possible that sentencing decisions of Murder cases rely heavily on legally based characters. It is for this reason that results indicate the significance of legal variables (e.g., level of seriousness of offense, prior number of offenses and strikes) in the sentencing of Murder cases.

Similar to the previous findings, Table 7 shows that when sentencing Robbery cases, race/ethnicity has no significant effect. Robbery, classified as a more serious offenses is comprised of factors which may be regarded as serious. For example, the use of weapon or physical harm to a victim during a Robbery may present a clear level of seriousness, thus not allowing any extra legal factors such as race/ethnicity in determining sentence length. In such cases, it is expected that race/ethnicity will not be a significant predictor in sentence length (Spohn & Cederblom, 1991). Legal variables (i.e., level of seriousness of offense, number of prior offenses, number of prior strikes) all significantly predict sentence length in Robbery cases. Interestingly, Jury trials have a significant effect on the sentencing of these cases. The significance of Jury trials may be attributed to the lack of willingness by defendants to accept a guilty plea. Defendants and their counsel may believe that a lack of overwhelming evidence exists and thus choose to have their case heard by a jury trial.

In accord with the liberation hypothesis, one would not expect race/ethnicity to be a significant predictor in the sentencing of Firearm related offenses due to the seriousness of the offense. The presence of a firearm during the commission of any strike offense clearly increases level of severity. In this analysis, race/ethnicity is not a significant predictor (Table 8). Once again, as results from the sentencing of Murder and Robbery cases revealed, judges may discard any extra legal variables due to the seriousness of the offense. While level of seriousness of offense, number of prior offenses, and number of prior strikes all have a positive effect, Guilty plea and Jury trials were insignificant in the sentencing of Firearm related offenses.

<u>Findings from Research Question 1c: Will race/ethnicity have a significant effect on the sentencing of assault, theft, drug, and residential burglary cases.</u>

Since Assault is considered a less serious felony offenses, the multivariate analysis results should feature significant effects for race/ethnicity variables. However, Table 9 indicates that only Asian offenders received a longer sentence than Whites for Assault cases. All legal variables are significant predictors of sentence length in these cases. Offenders who Plea guilty receive 11 months less than offenders who had a Bench trial in Assault cases.

Considered together, these results reveal minimal support for racial/ethnic disparity in sentencing decisions of less serious offenses such as Assault. The significance of legal variables indicates that their predictive power is not only confined to more serious offenses but also less serious offenses. Due to the sheer number of Assault cases, it is not surprising that defendants are offered plea arrangements which substantially reduces sentence length.

Results from the analysis on Theft cases reveal that the only racial/ethnic variable that significantly predicts total sentence in Theft cases is Native American offenders (Table 10). Number of counts, level of seriousness of offense, number of prior offenses, number of prior strikes, and Jury trials all have a positive effect in total sentence of Theft cases. These results on the sentencing of Theft cases once again reveal minimal support for racial/ethnic disparity among offenders sentenced of less serious offenses.

Assessment of the influence of race/ethnicity on Drug cases reveals that an offender's race/ethnicity is a significant predictor in sentences involving drug cases. However, the only significant racial/ethnic variable is Black offenders. More interestingly, this effect is negative. Thus, Black offenders receive 5 months shorter sentence than White offenders. This contradicts the liberation hypothesis which suggests that race/ethnicity is a significant predictor in less serious cases (i.e., drug cases). This may be a direct result of the lack of willingness by judges to increase incarceration rates with drug offenders. While legal variables have a positive effect in sentencing of Drug cases, Guilty plea and Jury trial cases are significant predictors in the expected direction. Thus, the sentence length of Drug cases is also determined by other legal variables. Judges may place considerable importance on the presence of prior offenses (including drug offenses) in determining sentence length for Drug cases.

In assessing Residential Burglary cases, there were no significant effects for race/ethnicity variables. One again, this is inconsistent with the liberation hypothesis. This result may be attributed to the level of seriousness attached to Residential Burglary offenses in Washington. While it may be regarded as a less serious offense, the Revised Code of Washington 9A.52.025 states that it should be considered a more serious offense than second degree Burglary. Therefore, judges may not allow extra legal variables such as race/ethnicity to influence sentence length decisions. Legal variables and Jury trials have a positive effect on sentence length for these cases. Offenders clearly do not benefit from choosing a Jury trial, since they receive over three years longer sentences than offenders who choose a Bench trial.

<u>Findings from Research Question 2a: Will race/ethnicity have a significant effect on above guideline departure for both strike and non-strike offense cases?</u>

In examining above guideline departures for strikes offenses, results indicate no significant effects of race/ethnicity (see Table 14). In fact, the only two significant predators are level of seriousness of offense and number of prior offenses. Clearly, other variables not included in this assessment are accounting for the variance in above guideline departure for strike offenses. These variables may include the presence of eyewitnesses, number of victims or whether victim(s) sustained substantial injuries.

When examining above guideline departures for non-strike offenses, Hispanic offenders have a negative effect on above guideline departures (see Table 15). Thus, Hispanic offenders on the average receive shorter sentences than White offenders. Interestingly, Hispanic offenders who receive below guideline departures for strike offenses obtain longer sentences than White offenders, however when they receive above guideline departures for non-strike offenses, they obtain shorter sentences than White offenders. This provides proof that an offender's race/ethnicity can have very different effects at different types of departures. Firearm related offenses significantly predict above guideline departures. This is consistent with the findings on overall guideline departure. Interestingly, level of seriousness of offense and number of prior offenses have a negative effect on above guideline departure for non-strike offenses.

<u>Findings from Research Question 2b: Will race/ethnicity have a significant effect on overall guideline departures?</u>

In measuring overall guideline departures, a negative coefficient indicates a negative effect on sentence length, thus a shorter sentence; a positive coefficient indicates a positive effect, thus a longer sentence. As hypothesized, race/ethnicity has no significant effect on overall guideline departure for strike offenses (Table 13a). This may be attributed to the inability to distinguish between different types of departures and thus not allowing to examine whether sentences depart below the minimum guideline or above the maximum guideline. Robbery, Assault, and Rape offenses are significant positive predictors of this departure. While these types of offenses significantly predict overall guideline departure, it is unknown whether they are significant at below or above guideline departures. This will be addressed in the subsequent analysis. As expected, weapon enhancement has a positive effect, while Guilty plea and Jury trial cases also have a significant effect.

For non-strike offenses, once again race/ethnicity is not a significant predictor of overall guideline departure 13b). However, it is possible that the effect of race/ethnicity may be significant in specific types of departures. The only non-strike offense that has a significant effect in these cases is Firearm related offenses. The positive effect of this offense indicates a longer sentence for those offenders sentenced for a Firearm related offense. This finding provides proof that Firearm related offenses are considered serious offenses and thus enhancing sentence length without the impact of race/ethnicity. Sex is a significant predictor of overall guideline departure for non-strike offenses, as is number of prior offenses and Jury trials. However, Guilty plea has a negative effect on overall guideline departure for non-strike offenses. Findings indicate that mode of disposition significantly predicts not only sentence length but also overall guideline departure. Unfortunately, these findings do not reveal whether the significance of this variable applies to different types of departures.

Findings from Research Question 2c: Will race/ethnicity have a significant effect on below guideline departures for both strike and non-strike offense cases?

When interpreting coefficients that predict below guideline departure, a negative coefficient indicates a longer sentence, while a positive coefficient indicates a shorter sentence. For strike offenses, Native American and Hispanic offenders receive longer sentence than White offenders for cases that received a below guidelines departure (Table 14). Thus, although these offenders receive a below guideline departure, they still received a longer sentence than White offenders. This provides moderate support for the argument that racial/ethnic disparity exists in sentencing decisions. Murder, Robbery, Assault, Rape, Other Sex Offenses, and Kidnapping offenses have a significant effect on below guideline departures. Offenders who are sentenced for these offenses receive longer sentences than those who commit any other non-strike offense (reference category). This finding indicates that while offenders sentenced for strike offenses received below minimum guideline sentences, they still received longer sentences than Non-strike offenses. Weapon enhancements also have a significant effect on below guideline departure.

For below guideline departures of non-strike offenses, Asian, Native American, and Hispanic offenders all have a significant effect on these departures (Table 15). These offenders received longer sentences than White offenders for non-strike offenses. This finding also provides moderate support for the argument that racial/ethnic disparity exists in sentencing decisions which fall below guideline requirements. Forgery, weapon enhancement, level of seriousness of offense, number of prior strikes and guilty plea also have a significant effect on below guideline departures. The significance of Forgery offenses may be a result of the less serious connotation attached by judges in making sentencing decisions. The assumption that crimes against property are punished in a severe manner is clearly not shown in these assessments.

Findings from Research Question 3: Will race/ethnicity have a significant effect on decision to Plea Bargain?

For strike offenses, the odds of modes of disposition resulting in a guilty plea for Black offenders are 1.5 times higher than for Whites (Table 16a). However, Hispanic offenders have a lower odds of receiving a guilty plea (.75 times lower). For non-strike offenses, the odds for Blacks are 1.5 times higher of having a guilty plea verdict, while .771 times lower for Hispanic offenders (Table 16b). These findings indicate that not all minority offenders are advised by counsel to accept a guilty plea. It is also possible that not all minority offenders are offered the opportunity to plea bargain a case.

Findings from Research Question 4: Will race/ethnicity have a significant effect on decisions to allocate Community Supervision?

The only significant race/ethnicity variable predicting community supervision is the variable for Black offenders. In strike offenses, the odds of Black offenders receiving community supervision are .781 times lower than for White offenders. In non-strike offenses, the odds for Blacks is .840 times lower than for Whites. This finding is surprising when one considers the disproportionate number of Black offenders who are under correctional supervision.

Event Sequence Analysis

The following section will present analyses for the event sequence data analysis regarding repeat and third strike offenders. First, focus will be given to the repeat offender sample, followed by an analysis of the group of third strike offenders. In order to examine the sequence of offenses committed by repeat offenders, probabilities for offenses are presented in Table 18 - 22. When assessing property offenses committed by White male offenders, analyses reveal that the probability of committing a Robbery offense at T1 and T2 is .315 (Table 18). Also, offenders sentenced for Theft offenses at T1 have a .249 probability of committing a subsequent Theft offense at T2. The probability of committing a Murder at T1 and T2 is .179 for White male offenders. Offenders sentenced for an Assault offense at T1 have a .250 probability of committing an Assault offense at T2. There were no significant probabilities for Drug offense sequences. Offenders sentenced for a Rape offense at T1 have a .261 probability of committing another Rape offense at T2. The probability is even higher for Other Sex Offenses. Offenders convicted of Other Sex Offenses have a .467 probability of committing another sex offense at T2. Considered together, these findings provided support for the specialization hypothesis among White male repeat offenders. This indicates that White males sentenced for a particular felony offenses will likely commit a similar subsequent offense.

White female offenders have a .500 probability of committing a Theft offense at T1 and a Robbery offense at T2 (Table 19). Interestingly, the probability of committing an Assault 1 or 2 at T1 and committing a Residential Burglary offense at T2 is .250. White female offenders thus tend to specialize in property offenses. More importantly, the sentencing of a Theft offense will likely result in the future sentencing of a Robbery offense, indicating a progression in seriousness of offenses. Specialization seems evident in the sentencing of personal offenses as well. The probability of committing an Assault 3 at T1 and an Assault 1 or 2 at T2 is .500. Unlike male offenders, White female offenders have a .409 probability of committing a Drug offense at T1 and T2.

Among Black male offenders, the probability of committing a Robbery offense at T1 and T2 is .294 (Table 20). The probability of committing a Theft at T1 and T2 is .274. Black male offenders like their White counterparts tend to be sentenced for subsequent similar property offenses. However, there is proof that offenders within this subsample commit different types of offenses over time. Among Black male offenders, committing a Burglary offense at T1 and an Assault 1 or 2 at T2 has a .500

probability of occurring, while the probability of committing an Assault 1 or 2 at T1 and a Drug offense at T2 is .208. Similar to the White females in the sample, Black males have a .442 probability of committing a Drug offense at both T1 and T2. Results indicate that while Black offenders tend to specialize when committing property and drug offenses, they also tend to be sentenced for personal offenses (Assault 1 or 2) after being sentenced for property offenses (Burglary) and sentenced for Drug offenses after the sentencing of an Assault 1 or 2.

Black female offenders convicted of a Robbery at T1 have a .800 probability of committing a Robbery at T2 (Table 21). While the probability of committing an Assault 1 or 2 at T1 and a Drug offense at T2 is .333, the probability that a Drug offense will be committed at T1 and T2 is .553. Based on these assessments, one could conclude that Black female offenders tend to specialize in the offenses for which they are sentenced. Consistent with the Black male repeat offenders, Black females also tend to follow an Assault offense with a Drug offense. These results provide proof that drug offenses follow and not precede other types of offenses. However, Black female offenders also tend to commit mixed offenses. Results indicate equal probabilities for offenders committing an Assault 3 at T1 and a Residential Burglary or Assault 3 at T2.

Hispanic male offenders have a .286 probability of committing a Murder at T1 and T2 (Table 22). This is the highest probability for subsequent Murder offenses in the samples examined. The probability of these offenders committing Murder offenses in sequence indicates how propensity towards serious violent offenses varies across racial/ethnic groups. The probability of committing similar subsequent property offenses and drug offenses also is revealed. For example, the probability of committing Robbery at T1 and T2 is .500, while the probability of committing a Drug offense at T1 and T2 is .333.

Findings from Pattern of Offenses Among Third Strike Offenders

White three strike offenders have an interesting sequence of offenses. When examining offenses committed at T1 and T2, we find that offenders have a .813 probability of committing Robbery offenses during these time periods (Table 23). Also, they have a .500 probability of committing an Assault at T1 and T2. These findings indicate that three strike offenders notably commit Robbery and Assault offenses for their first two strike offenses. For offenses committed during T2 and T3, results indicate that offenders have a .800 probability of committing a Rape offense if they committed a Rape at T2, while only a .333 probability from T1 to T2. Thus, Rape offenses tend to be committed at higher rates from T2 to T3 than from T1 to T2. White offenders once again have a high probability of committing a Robbery offense at T1 and T3 (.625).

During time periods T1 and T2, minority three strike offenders have a .455 probability of committing Assault offenses and a .815 probability of committing Robbery offenses (Table 24). The sentencing of Robbery offenses continues on to the third strike. For example, minority third strike offenders have a .667 probability of being sentenced for a Robbery at T2 and T3 and a .669 probability of being sentenced for a Robbery at T1 and T3. This reveals that the majority of White and minority third strike offenders tend to commit Robbery offenses. In reference to sex offenses, minority offenders tend to have a lower probability than White offenders of being sentenced for similar subsequent sex offenses.

Elite Interviews

The telephone interviews conducted with prosecutors and defense attorneys revealed insightful details regarding the processing of repeat offenders and third strike offenders. The prime objective of these interviews was to gain an informal understanding about the impact of the three strikes law at the level of policy implementation. While I contacted every prosecutor's office and assigned counsel office in the state, a total of only 32 interviews was conducted. Among these were 18 prosecutors, 13 defense attorneys, and the co-author of the third strike law in the state. The questions asked of the officials focused on the general impact felt from the implementation of the law, types of offenses which qualify as strike offenses, and the their general perception concerning the law.

General Impact of the Law

The interview with a co-author of the law, Mr. David LaCourse, revealed that the notion of a third strike law developed out of having been a victim of a serious crime. After being assaulted and experiencing a situation wherein an arrest never resulted, Mr. LaCourse began to conduct research on the number of arrests which follow an offense. He indicated the following:

> I was mugged and the perpetrator was never arrested. I found out that in the Seattle area 75% of

> violent assaults don't result in an arrest. By the time those 25% reach the end of the pipeline, how many are convicted for that violent assault? By the time they are put in prison how many offenses have they committed?

Mr. LaCourse stated that the focus of his personal research then became the development of a law which would target violent repeat offenders. While he indicated being familiar with the Washington Habitual Offender Law, he noted the following:

> The habitual offender law allowed the judge to waive a life sentence for offenders who should have been locked-up. This law was just too broad.

Mr. LaCourse proceeded by indicating that repeat offenders are still allowed the opportunity to avoid a life sentence if sentenced under the three strike law:

> The law provided the line in the sand. No more excuses, just convince the Governor that you should be given a pardon and that's it.

While California is often mistakenly identified as having created the three strikes law, it was indicated that the Washington law was instrumental in the development of California' law:

> When the creator of MADD called and asked for my advice they had adopted our model; however, once certain people got a hold of it, they thought our version was too narrow. We just figured that

> the people of Washington would not pay for non-violent offenses (Mr. La Course).

Interestingly, this statement gives the impression that maybe if the people of Washington were willing to pay for the long term incarceration of non-violent offenders, the list of offenses which comprises strikes would be expanded. This is contrary to the justification of the three strikes law which is based on the notion that only serious offenses should be included.

When respondents were asked to compare the Washington law with California's version, a consistent dissatisfaction was noted. For example, a prosecutor made the following statement:

> In California about 40 -75% of the strike offenses are non-violent. They did it all wrong. It is just too fiscally damaging.

Another prosecutor indicated the limited scope of the Washington law:

> California made a mistake by including every offense possible. Here it's narrow and it applies to people who commit crimes of violence.

Another respondent included the following observation:

> They'll feel it really bad in 2 or 3 years when all those two strikers come through again.

Respondents presented differing notions regarding the specific offenders that the law is affecting. For example, one public defender indicated:

> The offenders that we have processed are not violent, aggressive people but the people voted for the law and unfortunately, they didn't foresee the cases where it's difficult to call.

A prosecutor commented on the "type" of offenders which are being impacted:

> We need to realize that third strike offenders do not represent anyone, just offenders that have an average of 12 convictions.

Critics of the law often call attention to the anticipated reduction of plea bargaining which would result in a large proportion of offenders being less willing to plea bargain their case and thus choose a jury or bench trial. When respondents were asked to comment on this issue, two respondents (a prosecutor and the other a public defender) stated the following:

> Prosecutors are being tough since they are not letting those Robbery 2 cases fall down like they used to.
>
> Plea bargaining is still possible. A soft Robbery 2 can become a Theft 1, but Robbery 1 is more difficult to plea to Theft 1.

A public defender had a different perception of the impact on plea bargaining:

> My work now involves telling these guys that the prosecutors have no reason to offer them a deal. What do they gain? Before, they were willing to make a weapon disappear but now no way.

A specific prosecutor made it very clear that plea bargaining was not a mechanism used at random by prosecutors. He indicated great dissatisfaction with the notion that plea bargaining would no longer benefit offenders. He adds:

> Plea bargain has not disappeared. Offers are made every day. Here we have always plea bargained smart, that's why we have the numbers we have. Plea bargaining is not a loophole for anyone, and it hasn't gone away.

Various county officials indicated little or no impact felt by the law. For example, comments included:

> Our office has not been affected. The only difference was that we filed a notice indicating that they were third strike offenders.

> We have not done anything differently in these cases, the research and prep is the same.

> Here we have had two cases and have dismissed them so that Steven's county could take them.

Even a prosecutor in one of the largest counties in the state indicated little impact:

> Here we have had 27 cases with life with no parole. We keep our case load on track to know exactly where the repeat offenders are at. The only added work has been the added paper work to prove that the offender actually has two prior convictions.

Types of Offenses

In discussing the types of offenses which qualify as strikes, it is important to note the great variability in offense definition across the states. For example, the definition of personal versus property offenses differs across states. Public officials had differing perceptions regarding the offenses which are regarded as strike offenses. Some indicated:

> The definition of offenses varies from state to state. For example Burglary, in some, its a violent offense--in some, it's a property offense. Here, Burglary 1 is a personal offense. That makes a difference. Read the law.

Various respondents indicated the problems with classifying certain offenses as strikes:

> Are property offenders the type that we refer to when we think of third strike offenders? Of course not.

> We are seeing less repeat offenders, those are offenders that present a threat of violence to an individual not the property offenders.
>
> In the rural part of the state, we have some stealing which is not for fun and games. This is because people are poor. Were supposed to lock them up too?
>
> The problem comes with the Assault 2 cases. What about those cases where you have a knife but don't hit anyone? If the guy steals a soda and is charged with robbery, then you can't send that guy to jail for life.
>
> With violent crimes you always have the cutting edge crimes, like Assaults, Burglary, and Robbery.

Others indicated:

> A rape case or first degree robbery, we just proceed to prove it, and once sentenced then its not a big choice.
>
> Reckless endangerment is now drive-by shooting, which is clearly a violent offense. You drive-by with the intent to hurt someone.

While possession of an illegal substance is not a qualifying strike offense, other offenses are qualifying which are often involved in the distribution, manufacture or possession of an illegal substance. Officials indicated the following:

> Drug offenses are covered if you have a deadly weapon on you, not the simple possession of a drug. Some people don't know that.
>
> Drug cases where homicide results are taken care of in Manslaughter.
>
> Giving drugs to a minor is a class A felony, and by definition all class A felonies are violent crimes--but it's not and shouldn't be a strike.

An often noted comment was the problem with developing a list of offenses which will receive little criticism. As one official indicated:

> Language problems still exists but we can't please everyone, there will always be someone that is upset with a particular crime.

General Perceptions

Public officials' perceptions can be easily classified into two classifications, positive and negative. Moreover, prosecutors and public defenders also consistently fell into these expected classifications. For example, prosecutors indicated the following:

> I am encouraged by police officers and prison guards, they appreciate what we have done.
>
> Five years from now, fiscal concerns will be gone, because we still have 1/3 of what we expected.

> Worse of the worse, we are not getting right away, but they'll be back.
>
> We have offenders like (offender's name) who are three strike plus offenders who escaped the prosecuting of the third strike but are now on death row. These are the offenders we target.
>
> We have an offender who has four strikes, yet his current offense is not a strike--but he'll be back around.

Public defenders then indicated:

> It's a good policy if you commit three serious crimes but not for this stuff that can be classified as strike offenses like Assault 2.
>
> The law is a crock. Who are we kidding?
>
> The legislature is trying to micromanage the courts; this is a serious issues.
>
> To whom does it make sense to lock them up when they are in their late 30's?
>
> I hope that eventually judges are allowed some discretion with the long sentences.
>
> The concept of locking up offenders is a good one, but whether it works in reality is another issue.

One of the most interesting comments came from an official who was one of the few respondents who addressed the racial disproportionality issues. He notes:

> 99% of the convicted offenders are men, but you don't hear me saying that there are too many men being convicted.

Analyses in this chapter have attempted to capture the effect of race/ethnicity on decisions to sentence repeat offenders and third strike offenders. Assessments of the influence of race/ethnicity on total sentence reveals little support for race/ethnic bias in sentencing decisions. This finding is consistent with Griswold's (1987) examination of race/ethnicity and legal variables on sentencing decisions. Results indicate that only one of the four race/ethnic variables significantly predicts sentence length and thus receive longer sentences than Whites. The significant effect of Assault cases indicates how less serious offenses can be treated and handled as serious offenses. Legal variables as expected significantly predict sentence length. This is not a surprise since prior criminal record is always taken into account when making sentencing decisions.

The separate multivariate analysis for each type of offense revealed that race/ethnicity is an insignificant predictor in Murder, Robbery and Firearm related offenses. These findings are not surprising when one considers the seriousness of these offenses. Extra legal variables are irrelevant when sentencing these types of offenses. It is therefore not alarming that level of offenses seriousness, number of prior offenses and strikes all had a significant effect on the sentence length of these three offenses. In predicting the offense of Assault, the only significant race/ethnicity variable was Asian offenders. This evidence also provides minimal support for the argument that racial/ethnic bias exists in sentencing decisions. The significant effect of legal variables provides evidence that these indicators are not only important in the sentencing of more serious offenses but also in less serious offenses. In sentencing of Theft offenses, Native American offenders significantly predict this sentence. However, the other race/ethnicity variables were insignificant in this assessment.

Regarding the sentencing of Drug cases, interestingly, Black offenders have a negative effect on this sentence length. A shorter sentence for these offenders may be a result of judges not willing to incarcerate Drug offenders for long spans of time. When sentencing Residential Burglary offenses, results reveal no significant race/ethnicity variables. According to the liberation hypothesis, race/ethnicity should significantly predict the sentence length of less serious offenses such as Residential Burglary. However, the Washington statute on Residential Burglary clearly outlines the level of severity of this offense. The lack of predictability power of all race/ethnicity variables in these models of specific offenses does in fact, reveal the significant effect of legal variables (i.e., level of seriousness of offense, prior criminal history record, number of prior strike offenses). While as expected, race/ethnicity is not significant in the sentencing of serious offenses, there is minimal support for the argument that minority offenders are sentenced longer for less serious offenses.

Findings from the guideline departure analyses indicate, as hypothesized, race/ethnicity having no significant effect on overall guideline departure for strike and non-strike offenses. Similar to Griswold (1987), these findings indicate that legal variables such as type of offense, number of prior offenses, and mode of disposition have a significant effect on overall guideline departures. These findings unfortunately do not provide information on whether race/ethnicity is significant in different types of guideline departures.

Results from assessments on below guideline departure indicate that for strike offenses, Native American and Hispanic offenders receive longer sentences than White offenders and for non-strike offenses, Asian, Native American, and Hispanic offenders receive longer sentences than Whites. These results present some proof for the argument that racial/ethnic disparity exists when determining sentence decisions. While number of prior offenses does not have a significant effect on both strike and non-strike offenses, number of prior strikes significantly predicts below guideline departures in these cases. The predictive power of number of prior strikes gives rise to the question of which crime history variable is most appropriate in estimating sentencing decisions.

Above guideline departure results reveal that for strike offenses, no significant race/ethnicity variables predict this departure. However, for non-strike offenses Hispanic offenders in general, receive a shorter sentence than White offenders. These results indicate how race/ethnicity may have different effects at different types of departures. In both strike and non-strike cases, level of offense seriousness and number of prior offenses have a negative effect on above guideline departures. This finding is consistent with Kramer and Ulmer's (1996) finding that offense seriousness and number of prior offenses have a negative effect on above guideline departure. This effect is due to the large width of guideline cells where seriousness of offense and criminal history is extremely high.

Results on effect of race/ethnicity on Guilty plea reveal the importance of analyzing minority offenders into different racial/ethnic categories. Findings indicate that Black and Hispanic offenders have very different odds of receiving a guilty plea. Findings on the effect of race/ethnicity on community supervision indicate that Black offenders have odds lower than White offenders of receiving community supervision. This result is almost counterintuitive when one considers the number of Black offenders under correctional care.

While assessments of offense patterns often provide little support for the specialization of offenses committed by offenders (Wolfgang, Figlio, & Sellin, 1972; Kempf, 1987; Blumstein, Cohen, & Farrington, 1988), results on the sequence of offenses committed by repeat and third strike offenders reveal a pattern of homogeneity. This is especially true for Robbery, Assault, and Drug offenses. The only evidence that offenders tend to commit more serious subsequent offenses was present in the assessments of White female offenders. They have a significant probability if committing a Robbery offenses after committing a Theft offense. While there were significant probabilities involving mixed offenses, results clearly provide support for the assumption of specialization among these offenders. Thus, repeat offenders and third strike offenders tend to be specialists in their patterns of crime. This finding is consistent with findings on career criminals produced by Gottfredson and Gottfredson (1993).

Interviews with public officials provided context for the quantitative findings in this study. Interestingly, after five years of being implemented, the three strikes law effects are still producing varying reactions from officials responsible for processing third strike offenders. Clearly, there is immense disenchantment from public defenders and great satisfaction among prosecutors. Developments in years to come will undoubtedly capture the long term effects of the three strikes law. However, currently public officials are still making efforts to establishing some sort of stability and predictability in their courtrooms.

CHAPTER 6

Conclusion and Discussion

Any examination of crime control policy must be based on two fundamental concerns. First, the desire to obtain the most accurate representation of a crime problem, along with its most appropriate solution and second, to provide the most unbiased evaluations to the public. The creation and implementation of the three strikes law provided an appropriately simple solution to a crime problem—namely, life imprisonment for offenders convicted of three serious felonies. However, this solution also created an array of unanswered questions. For example, are counties and states prepared for the fiscal impacts of the law? Are all repeat offenders within the criminal justice system going to be affected by the law? How do we justify the inclusion of offenses that should be regarded as strikes? And lastly, how will we justify incarcerating offenders for life who will be disproportionately racial/ethnic minorities?

This present study on the sentencing of repeat offenders within Washington State provided an opportunity to explore several important research questions that not only inform policymakers but are also the focus of much sentencing research. By utilizing data from the State of Washington Sentencing Guidelines Commission on felony cases for years 1993 - 1997, it was possible to examine the effect of legal and extralegal indicators on cases where a "most serious offense" was involved. The focus of this study was to explore racial/ethnic impacts on sentences for different types of offenses and examine any possible sentencing guideline departures. Moreover, this study also examined the sequence of offenses committed by repeat and third strike offenders. Lastly, telephone interviews with courtroom personnel captured their general perceptions regarding the three strikes law.

A fundamental element in an analysis of judicial disparity is the determination of whether certain groups of offenders are being sentenced in a fashion similar to the "typical" offender. This is complicated by the different goals of punishment. As we know, judges must disentangle and balance these goals when making sentencing decisions. When measuring sentencing decisions, capturing as many factors as possible which can potentially influence sentencing decisions is crucial. While some studies have found that minority offenders receive longer sentences (Klepper, Nagin, & Tierney, 1983; Petersilia, 1983; Spohn, Delone, & Spears, 1998; Spohn, Gruhl, & Welch, 1981-1982; Steffensmeier & Demuth, 2000; Zatz, 1984), others argue that racial/ethnic disparity only appears when there are no appropriate statistical controls for legal criteria (Hagan, 1974; Kleck, 1981; Pruitt & Wilson, 1983; Kramer & Steffensmeier, 1993; Ulmer & Kramer, 1996). Given these conflicting findings, research should continue to examine both legal and extralegal variables in sentencing decisions.

Findings from this study show that the effect of race/ethnicity on sentence length provide minimal support for racial/ethnic bias in sentencing claims. Consistent with Spohn and Cederblom (1991), Murder, Rape, and Assault offenses were significant predictors of sentence length. Moreover, legal characteristics were significant predictors of sentence length. In order to further test the liberation hypothesis, separate examinations on the effect of race/ethnicity on sentence length for Murder, Robbery, Firearm Related Offenses, Assault, Theft, Drug offenses, and Residential Burglary cases were conducted. The findings observed indicate that the effect of race/ethnicity on less serious cases (i.e., Assault, Theft, Drug offenses) are minimal at best.

While race/ethnicity was not a significant predictor in Murder, Robbery, and Firearm Relate Offenses, Asian offenders do receive longer sentences than Whites in Assault cases, and Native American offenders receive longer sentences in Theft cases. Interestingly, contrary to the liberation hypothesis, Black offenders receive shorter sentences than White offenders in Drug cases. In these assessments, legal variables clearly had a significant effect on sentence length. Based on these findings, we one can conclude that not all minority offenders are sentenced in the same manner.

Although studies conducted by Moore and Miethe (1986) and Kramer and Steffensmeier (1993) found moderate evidence of racial disparity in sentencing decisions, Griswold (1987) found that legal variables do predict overall guideline departures to a substantial degree.

Results from the analysis on guideline departures reveal that race/ethnicity is a significant predictor mainly in below guideline departure cases. While receiving a below guideline departure may be of some benefit to all offenders without regard to minority status, this study sheds light on the fact that while minority offenders often receive a below guideline departure, they in fact are receiving longer sentences than Whites who also receive below guideline departures. The assumption that racial/ethnic disparity can only exist at the high end of guidelines departures is clearly not the case (see Kramer & Steffensmeier, 1993). It is possible for minority offenders to benefit at one end of the guideline departure, while being disadvantaged at the other. Whether disparity exists at one or both ends of the guideline departures continuum, a key element in that determination is the number of prior offenses committed by the offender. In fact, the number of prior strikes significantly influenced below guideline departures for both strike and non-strike offenses. In order to capture the types of offenses sentenced over time, this study also examined the sequence of offenses committed by these repeat offenders.

Findings observed on the sequence of offenses committed by repeat and third strike offenders reveal a rather clear pattern of specialization. This is especially true for Robbery, Assault, and Drug offenses. This finding is consistent with findings reported elsewhere on career criminals (Gottfredson & Gottfredson, 1993). Results also seem to be consistent across race/ethnic groups. While it is evident that within the state of Washington repeat and third strike offenders tend to be sentenced for similar offenses at least twice within their criminal careers, caution should be exercised in the interpretation of these results. Due to a lack of available data, analysis only included two time points for repeat offenders and three for the three strikes offenders. It is important to note that the offenses included in this study are regarded as the most serious types of offenses. Thus, this study provides information on the most feared criminal offender, the repeat violent offender. More importantly, the policy implications based on these results include the justification for laws designed to keep chronic offenders out of the public. For example, sex offender registration laws and weapon enhancements are clearly justified based on these results due to the high probability of offenders committing Robbery and Sex offenses over time. It should be noted that while previous studies have made efforts at establishing the escalation in seriousness of offenses, this assessment has captured the prevalence of repeat offenders committing serious felony offenses and not necessarily the escalation from non-felony to felony offenses.

Informal interviews with courtroom personnel who were directly involved in the sentencing process provided a candid look at the impact that three strikes law has had on courtroom cultures throughout the state. A key issue raised by these interviews was how the plea bargaining process became more unpredictable. According to interviews, it is much more difficult to predict the outcome of a repeat offender criminal case because prosecutors are less willing to plead down to a lesser degree offense. Moreover, according to these public officials, there is great uncertainty regarding how this law will impact crime. Surprisingly, at the time of the interviews the law in Washington State had been in effect for five years. Even after this time, the courtroom was still adapting to thee changes brought on by the law.

In sum, this study combined quantitative and qualitative methodologies to capture a comprehensive and insightful understanding of the Persistent Offender Accountability Act in Washington. The importance of this study lies in how it has identified important factors which are currently at play in the operation of three strikes laws. Findings from this study provided information which has yet to be addressed in the sentencing literature.

These results suggest the need for further examination of the relationship between racial/ethnic disparity and sentence length for specific offenses. Offenders presented in these analyses have been filtered through a process of numerous decisions and account for only offenders who have been sentenced for violent offenses. It is possible that the minimal effect that race/ethnicity has on these sentencing outcomes is a direct result of selection bias. Thus, race/ethnic differences that were present may have developed at earlier decision points. Future research should also address whether or not race/ethnic disparity exists within a sentencing guideline structure. The assumption that departures from sentencing schemes impact all offenders in a similar fashion is just not the case. Results from these analyses indicate that race/ethnicity can impact departures in different ways. Clearly, judicial discretion which allows for departures can sentence atypical cases. In sentencing those cases, judges can impose different standards and criteria. Ironically, this all occurs in a context where mechanisms have been created to abolish all possible disparities in the sentencing process. Further research on criminal careers can also expand what we know about habitual offender legislation.

Lastly, attention should be devoted towards identifying how the local context influences sentencing decisions. For example, how urbanization (see Myers & Talarico, 1986) and political culture influence departures. In examining case-processing decisions, focus on judges' decisions and courtroom culture. Also, attention to those decisions made earlier in case processing may shed light on sentencing outcomes. Much more research is needed to fully address the concerns raised by departures. By combining personal accounts from members of the courtroom culture and court specific information, much more can be discovered about the sentencing process.

Tables

Table 1. Descriptive Statistics for Continuous Variables

	N	Min.	Max.	M	SD
Age	19,403	13	81	30.3	10.06
Time	19,403	1	60	31.5	17.27
Counts	19,403	1	10	1.18	.60
Number of Prior Offenses	19,403	0	10	1.55	2.14
Number of Prior Strikes	19,403	0	10	.55	.65
Offense Seriousness	19,403	0	15	5.09	3.42
Sentence Length	19,403	.01	1,162	31.8	58.68
Below Departure	2,502	0	1	.53	.36
Above Departure	701	.00	14	.86	1.37
Overall Departure	18,211	-1	21.5	-.09	.56

Table 2. Number of Offenses by Race/Ethnicity, page1

			Race/ Ethnicity		
Strike Offense	White	Black	Asian	Nat Am.	Hisp.
Murder	290	110	9	16	32
Manslaughter	120	60	3	5	18
Robbery	1,405	599	60	63	104
Burglary	265	91	5	7	27
Assault	2,135	788	93	86	215
Rape	346	109	11	20	35
Other Sex Offense	1,539	437	48	63	125
Kidnapping	56	15	1	3	3
Vehicular Homicide	144	54	8	10	16
Other Strike Felony	392	132	10	11	46

Table 2. Number of Offenses by Race/Ethnicity (continued)

	Race/ Ethnicity				
Non-strike Offense	White	Black	Asian	Nat. Am.	Hisp.
Firearm	205	98	4	13	13
Assault 3	285	111	12	14	23
Residential Burglary	529	198	24	24	43
Theft	591	230	12	28	40
TMVWP	190	80	6	4	17
Possession Stolen Property	82	23	7	6	11
Forgery	262	90	7	9	21
Drug Offense	1,540	730	43	64	159
Other Non- Strike	1,604	579	43	67	152

Table 3. Frequencies of Mode of Disposition, Weapon Involvement, and Community Supervision

	Race/ Ethnicity				
	White	Black.	Asian	Nat. Am.	Hisp.
Sex					
Male	11,416 (94%)	4,201 (91%)	406 (96%)	465 (88%)	1,088 (98%)
Female	703 (6%)	402 (9%)	15 (4%)	61 (12%)	25 (2%)
Plead Guilty					
Yes	10,808 (90%)	3,949 (87%)	360 (88%)	476 (93%)	1,022 (93%)
No	1,189 (10%)	592 (13%)	46 (12%)	38 (7%)	79 (7%)
Jury Trial					
Yes	1,024 (8.5%)	520 (11%)	48 (12%)	38 (7%)	69 (6%)
No	11,125 (91.5%)	4,091 (89%)	373 (88%)	489 (93%)	1,048 (94%)
Weapon					
Yes	675 (5.6%)	284 (6%)	68 (16.7%)	34 (7%)	89 (8%)
No	11,322 (94.4%)	4,257 (94%)	480 (83.3%)	480 (93%)	1,012 (91%)
Comm. Supervision					
Yes	9,215 (77%)	3,461 (77%)	320 (79%)	390 (76%)	903 (82%)
No	2,782 (23%)	1,080 (23%)	86 (21%)	124 (24%)	198 (18%)

Table 4. Frequencies of Sentence Departures Above the Maximum Recommended and Below the Minimum Recommended by Offense*, page 1

	Departure Below	Overall Range	Departure. Above
Murder	51 (10.5%)	414 (85.5%)	19 (3.9%)
Manslaughter	26 (11.9%)	180 (82.6%)	12 (5.5%)
Robbery	274 (11.5%)	2,044 (85.9%)	62 (2.6%)
Burglary	41 (9.9%)	365 (87.7%)	10 (2.4%)
Assault	393 (11.2%)	2,993 (85.1%)	132 (3.8%)
Rape	62 (11.3%)	464 (84.8%)	21 (3.8%)
Other Sex Offense	450 (19.3%)	1,779 (76.1%)	108 (4.6%)
Kidnapping	15 (18.5%)	64 (79.0%)	2 (2.5%)
Vehicular Homicide	31 (12.4%)	210 (83.7%)	10 (4.0%)
Other Strike Felony	89 (14.0%)	521 (82.2%)	24 (3.8%)

* Within offense percentages are in parentheses

Table 4. Frequencies of Sentence Departures Above the Maximum Recommended and Below the Minimum Recommended by Offense (continued)

	Departure Below	Overall Range	Departure Above
Firearm	32 (9.1%)	302 (85.8%)	18 (5.1%)
Assault 3	62 (13.1%)	395 (83.5%)	16 (3.4%)
Residential Burglary	105 (12.2%)	728 (84.6%)	28 (3.3%)
Theft	110 (11.6%)	796 (84.0%)	42 (4.4%)
Motor Vehicle Theft	40 (12.9%)	255 (82.3%)	15 (4.8%)
Possession of Stolen Property	18 (13.1%)	117 (85.4%)	2 (1.5%)
Forgery	55 (13.3%)	344 (83.5%)	13 (3.2%)
Drug Offense	345 (12.8%)	2,260 (84.1%)	81 (3.0%)
Other Non-Strike	298 (11.5%)	2,211 (85.2%)	85 (3.3%)
Total	2,497 (12.7%)	16,452 (83.7%)	700 (3.6%)

* Within offense percentages are in parentheses

Table 5. Regression Analyses of Prison Term (in months) as Dependent Variable

Independent Variable	b	S.E.	(B)
Intercept	-52.720	3.062	
Age	-.185*	.030	-.032
Sex	-1.591	1.196	-.007
Black	-.101	.702	-.001
Asian	5.440*	1.985	.014
Native American	.989	1.775	.003
Hispanic	-1.763	1.254	-.007
Time	.053*	.017	.016
Counts	13.569*	.488	.142
Offense			
Murder 1 and 2	23.826*	1.904	.076
Manslaughter	-29.710*	3.354	-.053
Robbery	-3.741*	.789	-.025
Assault 1 and 2	4.049*	.701	.031
Burglary	-4.377*	2.039	-.011
Rape 1,2, and 3	4.2950*	1.405	.016
Other Sex Offense	-4.717*	.949	-.026
Kidnapping	-2.539	4.503	-.003
Vehicular Homicide	-5.517*	2.628	-.011
Other Strike	-1.021	1.676	-.003
Weapon	21.213*	1.240	.088
Level of Seriousness	11.508*	.096	.673
Prior Number of Offenses	5.377*	.145	.223
Prior Number of Strikes	14.229*	.558	.154
Guilty Plea	-8.060*	2.442	-.042
Jury Trial	18.827*	2.613	.092
N=	18,449		
R^2=	.532		

* $p < .05$

Table 6. The Effect of Race/Ethnicity on Sentencing Decisions in Murder Cases

Independent Variable	b	S.E.	(B)
Intercept	-73.497	26.057	
Age	-.295	.259	-.029
Sex	2.493	11.307	.006
Black	.952	5.950	.004
Asian	22.242	18.042	.031
Native American	18.517	14.056	.033
Hispanic	-7.844	9.622	-.021
Time	-.557*	.165	-.096
Counts	22.547*	4.615	.122
Weapon	26.432*	10.924	.062
Level of Seriousness	17.712*	.760	.729
Prior Number of Offenses	6.108*	1.266	.141
Prior Number of Strikes	29.925*	5.356	.164
Guilty Plea	-13.085	18.864	-.046
Jury Trial	22.638	19.914	.076
N=	656		
R^2=	.607		

* $p < .05$

Table 7. The Effect of Race/Ethnicity on Sentencing Decisions in Robbery Cases

Independent Variable	b	S.E.	(B)
Intercept	-59.929	5.630	
Age	.033	.058	.006
Sex	.061	2.003	.000
Black	-.507	1.192	.005
Asian	3.031	3.179	.011
Native American	-1.094	3.106	-.004
Hispanic	-2.839	2.609	-.012
Time	.183*	.032	.064
Counts	15.199*	.827	.204
Weapon	28.214*	2.544	.125
Level of Seriousness	10.076*	.184	.632
Prior Number of Offenses	5.175*	.256	.258
Prior Number of Strikes	9.237*	.792	.148
Guilty Plea	-6.528	4.543	-.039
Jury Trial	12.488*	4.876	.069
N=	3,400		
R^2=	.593		

* $p < .05$

Table 8. The Effect of Race/Ethnicity on Sentencing Decisions in Firearm Cases

Independent Variable	b	S.E.	(B)
Intercept	-48.401	27.678	
Age	-.239	.200	-.046
Sex	-2.908	7.607	-.015
Black	-6.102	4.425	-.056
Asian	8.131	17.959	.018
Native American	-5.700	9.771	-.022
Hispanic	-11.074	10.129	-.041
Time	.034	.117	.011
Counts	11.513*	4.318	.101
Weapon	27.571*	7.633	.140
Level of Seriousness	11.754*	.641	.768
Prior Number of Offenses	4.122*	.913	.204
Prior Number of Strikes	24.572*	4.059	.280
Guilty Plea	-7.605	24.264	-.042
Jury Trial	-7.537	25.147	-.041
N=	330		
R^2=	.563		

* $p < .05$

Table 9. The Effect of Race/Ethnicity on Sentencing Decisions in Assault Cases

Independent Variable	b	S.E.	(B)
Intercept	-53.195	5.440	
Age	-.175*	.050	-.033
Sex	.692	2.002	.003
Black	1.887	1.215	.015
Asian	5.592*	2.825	.019
Native American	-.150	2.960	.000
Hispanic	-.266	1.605	-.001
Time	-.014	.031	-.004
Counts	17.467*	.889	.183
Weapon	14.744*	2.280	.061
Level of Seriousness	12.534*	.184	.661
Prior Number of Offenses	5.050*	.264	.211
Prior Number of Strikes	10.388*	979	.116
Guilty Plea	-11.065*	4.447	-.061
Jury Trial	6.975	4.717	.036
N=	5,077		
R^2=	.571		

*$p < .05$

Table 10. The Effect of Race/Ethnicity on Sentencing Decisions in Theft Cases

Independent Variable	b	S.E.	(B)
Intercept	-79.959	18.775	
Age	.106	.156	.017
Sex	2.334	6.026	.010
Black	.087	3.605	.001
Asian	14.564	13.352	.027
Native American	35.660*	8.844	.100
Hispanic	3.275	7.594	.011
Time	-.137	.093	-.038
Counts	19.167*	3.083	.160
Weapon	6.245	6.914	.023
Level of Seriousness	10.973*	.538	.592
Prior Number of Offenses	5.476*	.707	.223
Prior Number of Strikes	12.254*	2.961	.121
Guilty Plea	11.319	16.242	.049
Jury Trial	59.335*	17.173	.243
N=	892		
R^2=	.469		

*p < .05

Table 11. The Effect of Race/Ethnicity on Sentencing Decisions in Drug Cases

Independent Variable	b	S.E.	(B)
Intercept	-42.395	7.798	
Age	-.182*	.084	-.031
Sex	-2.369	3.074	-.011
Black	-5.541*	1.867	-.045
Asian	2.410	6.213	.006
Native American	-4.519	5.146	-.013
Hispanic	-3.516	3.334	-.015
Time	.056	.048	.017
Counts	10.514*	1.531	.099
Weapon	22.715*	3.377	.098
Level of Seriousness	11.055*	.263	.658
Prior Number of Offenses	5.837*	.392	.247
Prior Number of Strikes	14.724*	1.549	.158
Guilty Plea	-12.464*	6.186	-.067
Jury Trial	16.130*	6.711	.079
N=	2,529		
R^2=	.500		

* $p < .05$

Table 12. The Effect of Race/Ethnicity on Sentencing Decisions in Residential Burglary Cases

Independent Variable	b	S.E.	(B)
Intercept	-73.715	15.522	
Age	.173	.138	.031
Sex	5.112	5.665	.022
Black	-2.221	3.165	-.017
Asian	-2.219	7.972	-.007
Native American	-7.856	8.071	-.024
Hispanic	3.248	6.017	.013
Time	.051	.077	.017
Counts	14.480*	2.028	.175
Weapon	25.128*	6.242	.102
Level of Seriousness	10.582*	.471	.613
Prior Number of Offenses	4.413*	.617	.201
Prior Number of Strikes	11.775*	2.559	.132
Guilty Plea	2.958	13.401	.016
Jury Trial	38.033*	14.127	.201
N=	817		
R^2=	.530		

*p < .05

Table 13a. Regression Models of Overall Sentencing Departure For Strike Offenses

Independent Variable	b	S.E.	(B)
Intercept	-.114	.044	
Age	-.002*	.000	-.049
Sex	.066*	.017	.029
Black	-.017	.010	-.013
Asian	.031	.028	.008
Native American	.043	.025	.013
Hispanic	-.016	.018	-.007
Time	.000*	.000	.015
Counts	.052*	.007	.057
Offense			
Murder	.051	.027	.017
Manslaughter	.020	.048	.004
Robbery	.033*	.011	.023
Assault	.084*	.010	.067
Burglary	.004	.029	.001
Rape	.105*	.020	.041
Other Sex Offense	-.018	.014	-.010
Kidnapping	.004	.064	.001
Vehicular Homicide	.017	.037	.003
Other Strike Offense	.034	.024	.011
Weapon	.100*	.017	.044
Level of Seriousness	-.000	.001	-.002
Prior Number of Offenses	.017	.002	.072
Prior Number of Strikes	.005	.008	.006
Guilty Plea	-.135*	.035	-.075
Jury Trial	.076*	.037	.039
N=	17,315		
R^2=	.035		

* $p < .05$

Table 13b. Regression Models of Overall Sentencing Departure For Non-Strike Offenses

	b	S.E.	(B)
Intercept	-.067	.044	
Age	-.002*	.000	-.052
Sex	.069*	.017	.030
Black	-.015	.010	-.011
Asian	.041	.029	.011
Native American	.045	.026	.013
Hispanic	-.008	.018	-.004
Time	.000*	.000	.021
Counts	.052*	.007	.058
Offense			
Firearm	.128*	.032	.030
Assault 3	.009	.027	.003
Residential Burglary	-.017	.021	-.006
Theft	.013	.020	.005
TMVWP	.019	.035	.004
Possession Stolen Property	-.035	.051	-.005
Forgery	-.002	.030	-.001
Drug	-.022	.012	-.014
Weapon	.086*	.017	.038
Level of Seriousness	-.001	.001	-.007
Prior Number of Offenses	.015*	.002	.065
Prior Number of Strikes	-.004	.008	-.005
Guilty Plea	-.138*	.035	-.076
Jury Trial	.080*	.037	.042
N=	17,315		
R^2=	.030		

*p < .05

Table 14a. Regression Models of Below Sentencing Departure For Strike Offenses

Independent Variable	B	S.E.	(B)
Intercept	-.026	.056	
Age	.002*	.000	.078
Sex	-.006	.018	-.005
Black	-.026	.015	-.027
Asian	-.068	.041	-.024
Native American	-.085*	.030	-.040
Hispanic	-.075*	.021	-.051
Time	.002*	.000	.101
Counts	.017	.011	.021
Offense			
Murder	-.150*	.036	-.072
Manslaughter	.090	.061	.025
Robbery	-.068*	.016	-.064
Assault	-.104*	.013	-.118
Burglary	-.013	.040	-.005
Rape	-.069*	.028	-.035
Other Sex Offense	.060*	.015	.065
Kidnapping	-.152*	.066	-.032
Vehicular Homicide	.095	.049	.027
Other Strike Offense	-.007	.028	-.004
Weapon	-.193*	.030	-.093
Level of Seriousness	.059	.002	.575
Prior Number of Offenses	-.000	.004	-.004
Prior Number of Strikes	-.079*	.013	-.119
Guilty Plea	.127*	.048	.076
Jury Trial	.007	.055	.004
N=	2,369		
R^2=	.534		

* $p < .05$

Table 14b. Regression Models of Above Sentencing Departure For Strike Offenses

Independent Variable	B	S.E.	(B)
Intercept	1.925	.490	
Age	.000	.005	.008
Sex	-.043	.247	-.007
Black	-.048	.148	-.013
Asian	.185	.336	.022
Native American	.419	.355	.046
Hispanic	-.381	.206	-.074
Time	-.005	.003	-.074
Counts	.027	.056	.019
Offense			
Murder	-.126	.333	-.019
Manslaughter	-.159	.523	-.015
Robbery	-.081	.161	-.020
Assault	.050	.126	.017
Burglary	-.126	.438	-.011
Rape	-.038	.205	-.007
Other Sex Offense	-.121	.152	-.032
Kidnapping	-.299	.952	-.012
Vehicular Homicide	-.342	.431	-.031
Other Strike Offense	.332	.305	.043
Weapon	-.109	.184	-.023
Level of Seriousness	-.063*	.016	-.178
Prior Number of Offenses	-.085*	.027	-.149
Prior Number of Strikes	-.092	.097	-.043
Guilty Plea	-.336	.326	-.108
Jury Trial	.069	.332	.021
N=	662		
R^2=	.067		

* $p < .05$

Table 15a. Regression Models of Below Sentencing Departure For Non- Strike Offenses

Independent Variable	b	S.E.	(B)
Intercept	-.066	.057	
Age	.002*	.000	.085
Sex	-.003	.019	-.003
Black	-.028	.015	-.029
Asian	-.087*	.042	-.030
Native American	-.100*	.031	-.047
Hispanic	-.086*	.022	-.058
Time	.001*	.000	.069
Counts	.016	.011	.020
Offense			
Firearm	-.035	.047	-.011
Assault 3	-.035	.034	-.015
Residential Burglary	-.008	.027	-.005
Theft	.015	.026	.009
TMVWP	-.041	.041	-.015
Stolen Property	-.067	.064	-.015
Forgery	.072*	.036	.029
Drug	.012	.015	.012
Weapon	-.189*	.031	-.090
Level of Seriousness	.063*	.002	.610
Prior Number of Offenses	-.003	.004	-.010
Prior Number of Strikes	-.054*	.014	-.081
Guilty Plea	.122*	.049	.073
Jury Trial	-.024	.056	-.013
N=	2,369		
R^2=	.507		

* $p < .05$

Table 15b. Regression Models of Above Sentencing Departure For Non- Strike Offenses

Independent Variable	b	S.E.	(B)
Intercept	1.838	.475	
Age	.000	.005	.007
Sex	-.044	.244	-.007
Black	-.018	.146	-.005
Asian	.211	.336	.025
Native American	.403	.354	.044
Hispanic	-.389*	.201	-.075
Time	-.005	.003	-.072
Counts	.029	.056	.021
Offense			
Firearm	1.036*	.329	.121
Assault 3	.092	.350	.010
Residential Burglary	-.172	.268	-.025
Theft	.115	.225	.020
TMVWP	-.029	.363	-.003
Stolen Property	-.252	.966	-.010
Forgery	.495	.376	.051
Drug	.196	.169	.046
Weapon	-.121	.181	-.026
Level of Seriousness	-.068*	.016	-.191
Prior Number of Offenses	-.093*	.026	-.164
Prior Number of Strikes	-.093	.096	-.043
Guilty Plea	-.303	.320	-.097
Jury Trial	.049	.327	.049
N=	662		
R^2=	.081		

* $p < .05$

Table 16a. Logistic Regression with Guilty Plea as a Dependent Variable for Strike Offenses

Independent Variable	b	S.E.	Odds
Intercept	2.195	.668	
Age	-.018*	.002	.982
Sex	.172	.116	1.187
Black	.413*	.058	1.511
Asian	.063	.166	1.065
Native American	-.242	.176	.785
Hispanic	-.290*	.124	.748
Time	.004	.002	1.004
Counts	-0.239*	.032	.788
Offense			
Murder	.262	.142	1.300
Manslaughter	.001	.253	1.001
Robbery	-.081	.070	.923
Assault	.208*	.061	1.232
Burglary	.162	.165	1.176
Rape	.609*	.098	1.838
Other Sex Offense	-.057	.082	.944
Kidnapping	.172	.359	1.187
Vehicular Homicide	.063	.225	1.065
Other Strike Offense	.460	.145	1.173
Weapon	1.102*	.079	3.009
Level of Seriousness	-.221*	.007	.802
Prior Number of Offenses	-.104*	.012	.901
Prior Number of Strikes	-.150*	.035	.861
N=	18,715		
Chi-square; df	1,639;22		

* $p < .05$

Table 16b. Logistic Regression with Guilty Plea as a Dependent Variable for Non-Strike Offenses

Independent Variable	b	S.E.	Odds
Intercept	3.997	.636	
Age	-.018*	.002	.982
Sex	.190	.116	1.209
Black	.419*	.058	1.521
Asian	.059	.166	1.061
Native American	-.225	.176	.799
Hispanic	-.261*	.124	.771
Time	.004*	.002	1.004
Counts	-.239*	.032	.788
Offense			
Firearm	-.120	.201	.887
Assault 3	-.021	.172	.950
Residential Burglary	.015	.125	1.015
Theft	-.206	.132	.814
TMVWP	-.194	.231	.824
Stolen Property	.371	.281	1.449
Forgery	-.200	.194	.819
Drug	-.040	.075	.961
Weapon	1.061*	.079	2.890
Level of Seriousness	-.221*	.007	.801
Prior Number of Offenses	-.102*	.012	.903
Prior Number of Strikes	-.139*	.035	.870
N=	18,715		
Chi-square; df	1,473; 20		

* $p < .05$

Table 17a. Logistic Regression with Community Supervision as a Dependent Variable for Strike Offenses

Independent Variable	b	S.E.	Odds
Intercept	2.432	.561	
Age	.015*	.002	1.015
Sex	-.092	.077	.912
Black	-.247*	.045	.781
Asian	.176	.133	1.192
Native American	.068	.114	1.070
Hispanic	-.068	.087	.935
Time	.002	.001	1.002
Counts	-.306*	.029	.737
Offense			
Murder	-.242	.132	.785
Manslaughter	1.192*	.204	3.295
Robbery	.945*	.046	2.574
Assault	-.403*	.048	.668
Burglary	.628*	.119	1.874
Rape	-.857*	.116	.424
Other Sex Offense	-.248*	.065	.780
Kidnapping	-.414	.342	.661
Vehicular Homicide	.837*	.149	2.308
Other Strike Offense	.231*	.104	1.260
Weapon	-2.248*	.162	.106
Level of Seriousness	-.012	.006	.990
Prior Number of Offenses	-.292*	.009	.747
Prior Number of Strikes	-.239*	.031	.788
Guilty Plea	-.041*	.066	.960
N=	18,715		
Chi-square; df	5,290; 23		

* $p < .05$

Table 17b. Logistic Regression with Community Supervision as a Dependent Variable for Non-Strike Offenses

Independent Variable	b	S.E.	Odds
Intercept	4.332	.490	
Age	.018*	.002	1.018
Sex	-.163*	.075	.849
Black	-.174*	.044	.840
Asian	.198	.129	1.219
Native American	.071	.111	1.074
Hispanic	-.136	.085	.873
Time	.002	.001	1.002
Counts	-.294*	.029	.746
Offense			
Firearm	.037	.137	1.038
Assault 3	.172	.114	1.187
Residential Burglary	.176*	.086	1.193
Theft	.073	.084	1.076
TMVWP	-0.76	.148	.925
Stolen Property	-.337	.246	.714
Forgery	-.224	.134	.799
Drug	-.278*	.057	.757
Weapon	-2.202*	.160	.111
Level of Seriousness	-.019*	.006	.982
Prior Number of Offenses	-.289*	.008	.749
Prior Number of Strikes	-.251*	.029	.778
Guilty Plea	.027	.064	1.027
N=	18,715		
Chi-square; df	3,397;21		

* $p < .05$

Table 18. Probabilities for Sequence of Offenses Among White Male Repeat Offenders

	Murder	Robbery	Assault 1 & 2	Rape	Other Sex Offense	Theft	Drug
Murder	.179*	-	-	-	-	-	-
Robbery	-	.315*	-	-	-	-	-
Burglary	-	.200	-	-	-	-	-
Assault 1 and 2	-	-	.250*	-	-	-	-
Rape	-	-	-	.261*	-	-	-
Other Sex Offense	-	-	-	-	.467*	-	-
Firearm Offense	-	-	-	-	-	-	.219
Assault 3	-	-	.313	-	-	-	-
Theft	-	-	-	-	-	.248*	-
Drug	-	-	.136	-	-	-	-

N = 1,110; * $p < .05$

Table 19. Probabilities for Sequence of Offenses Among White Female Repeat Offenders

	Robbery	Assault 1 and 2	Residential Burglary	Theft	Drug
Robbery	.250	-	-	.250*	-
Assault 1 and 2	-	-	.250*	-	-
Assault 3	-	.500*	-	-	-
Theft	.500*	-	-	-	-
Drug	-	-	-	-	.409*

N = 52;* p < .05

Table 20. Probabilities for Sequence of Offenses Among Black Male Repeat Offenders

	Murder	Robbery	Assault 1 and 2	Theft	Drug
Murder	.118*	.118	.118	-	.118
Robbery	-	.294*	-	-	-
Burglary	-	-	.500*	-	-
Assault1 and 2	-	-	-	-	.208*
Rape	-	-	.233	-	-
Other Sex Offense	-	.200	-	-	-
Firearm Related Offense	-	-	-	-	.333
Assault 3	-	-	.268*	-	-
Theft	-	-	-	.274*	-
Drug	-	-	-	-	.442*

N = 819;* $p < .05$

Table 21. Probabilities for Sequence of Offenses Among Black Female Repeat Offenders

	Robbery	Assault 3	Residential Burglary	Theft	Drug
Robbery	.800*	-	-	-	-
Burglary	.500	-	-	.500	-
Assault 1 and 2	-	-	-	-	.333*
Assault 3	-	.333*	.333*	-	-
Theft	.218	-	-	-	-
Drug	-	-	-	-	.553*

N = 75;* $p < .05$

Table 22. Probabilities for Sequence of Offenses Among Hispanic Male Repeat Offenders

	Murder	Robbery	Assault 1 and 2	Assault 3	Residential Burglary	Theft	Drug
Murder	.286*	-	-	-	-	-	-
Robbery	-	.500*	-	-	-	-	-
Burglary	-	-	.500	-	-	-	-
Assault 1 and 2	-	-	.235	-	-	-	.235
Rape	-	-	-	.400*	-	-	.400
Firearm Offense	-	-	-	-	-	.333*	.333
Assault 3	-	-	.300	-	-	-	-
Theft	-	-	-	-	.250*	.250*	-
Drug	-	-	-	-	-	-	.333*

N = 110;* $p < .05$

Table 23. Probabilities for Sequence of Offenses Among White Three Strike Offenders

		Murder	Assault	Robbery	Burglary	Rape
T1 to T2	Assault	-	.500*	-	-	-
	Robbery	-	-	.813*	-	-
	Burglary	-	-	-	.500*	-
	Rape	-	-	-	-	.333*
T2 to T3	Murder	.250	-	-	-	-
	Assault	-	.308	-	-	-
	Robbery	-	-	.719*	-	-
	Rape	-	-	-	-	.800*
T1 to T3	Assault	-	.286	.268	-	-
	Robbery	-	-	.625*	-	-
	Burglary	-	-	.500*	-	-
	Rape	-	-	-	.667	-

N = 60;* $p < .05$

Table 24. Probabilities for Sequence of Offenses Among Minority Three Strike Offenders

		Murder	Assault 1 and 2	Robbery	Rape
T1 to T2	Assault 1 and 2	-	.455*	-	-
	Robbery	-	-	.815*	-
	Rape	-	.500*	-	-
T2 to T3	Assault 1 and 2	.300*	.300	-	-
	Robbery	-	-	.667*	-
	Rape	-	.400	-	.400*
T1 to T3	Assault 1 and 2	-	.273	-	-
	Robbery	-	.185	.669*	-

N = 45;* $p < .05$

Appendix A: Correlation Matrix of Variables Included in Analyses

		1	2	3	4	5	6	7	8	9	10	11	12
TIME	(1)												
SEX	(2)	-0.025											
RACE1	(3)	-0.009	0.034										
RACE2	(4)	-0.003	-0.054	-0.769									
RACE3	(5)	0.011	0.018	-0.201	-0.083								
RACE4	(6)	0.002	-0.036	-0.227	-0.094	-0.017							
RACE5	(7)	0.016	0.043	-0.337	-0.141	-0.032	-0.037						
AGE	(8)	0.004	0.001	0.081	-0.033	-0.067	-0.013	-0.056					
GPLEA	(9)	0.017	-0.023	0.027	-0.049	-0.004	0.017	0.026	-0.054				
PSTRIKE	(10)	0.026	0.051	-0.065	0.133	-0.051	-0.01	-0.071	0.018	-0.005			
COUNTS	(11)	0.026	0.023	0.039	-0.022	-0.01	-0.011	-0.026	-0.005	-0.082	0.058		
TOTALSENT	(12)	0.004	0.041	-0.005	0.009	0.025	-0.006	-0.019	-0.006	-0.31	0.057	0.199	
MANSLAU	(13)	0.001	-0.002	-0.014	0.011	-0.006	-0.002	0.012	0.007	-0.014	-0.017	-0.009	0
BURGLARY	(14)	-0.007	-0.01	0.008	-0.005	-0.005	-0.007	0.006	-0.006	-0.008	0.009	0.006	0.004
OTHSEXOF	(15)	-0.048	0.014	0.037	-0.039	-0.002	0.001	-0.005	0.059	0.002	-0.036	-0.009	0.003
KIDNAP	(16)	0.008	0	0.009	-0.008	0.001	0.004	-0.006	0.012	-0.006	-0.006	-0.002	-0.002
VEHHOMIC	(17)	-0.003	-0.013	-0.006	-0.003	0.009	0.013	0.004	0.001	0.001	-0.019	-0.006	-0.005
OTHERSTR	(18)	0.002	-0.003	0.006	-0.008	-0.007	-0.009	0.013	0.01	0.002	-0.017	0.001	-0.016
FIREARM	(19)	0.027	0	-0.008	0.015	-0.01	0.009	-0.012	-0.014	0.004	0.011	-0.012	-0.003
ASSAULT3	(20)	0.019	-0.005	-0.004	0.003	0.007	0.003	-0.004	0.006	0.007	0.011	0.002	-0.008
RESBURG	(21)	-0.018	0.005	0.001	-0.002	0.011	0.001	-0.007	-0.021	0	0.034	0.006	-0.003
THEFT	(22)	-0.009	-0.004	0.005	0.005	-0.014	0.004	-0.015	0.002	0.018	0.03	-0.004	-0.013
TMVWP	(23)	0	0.011	-0.002	0.007	-0.002	-0.011	-0.001	-0.007	0.012	0.015	-0.007	-0.013
STOLPROP	(24)	0.006	0.014	-0.001	-0.013	0.018	0.009	0.009	-0.007	-0.005	0.004	-0.002	-0.01

Appendix A: Correlation Matrix of Variables Included in Analyses (continued)

		1	2	3	4	5	6	7	8	9	10	11	12
FORGERY	(25)	0.007	-0.009	0.009	-0.005	-0.005	-0.005	-0.004	0.002	0.008	0.021	0.03	-0.01
DRUG	(26)	0.03	-0.013	-0.032	0.039	-0.015	-0.008	0.006	-0.002	0.006	0.028	-0.008	-0.01
BELOWDEP	(27)	0.074	0.07	0.245	-0.209	-0.058	-0.07	-0.064	0.223	0.06	-0.421	0.006	-0.179
ABOVEDEP	(28)	-0.053	-0.014	0.039	-0.036	0.016	0.067	-0.065	0.011	-0.043	-0.07	-0.004	0.13
WEAPON	(29)	0.025	0.014	-0.032	0	0.064	0.003	0.021	-0.055	-0.127	-0.077	0.05	0.153
POFFENSES	(30)	0.07	0.03	-0.061	0.126	-0.055	-0.011	-0.066	0.004	-0.031	0.256	0.073	0.108
LEVEL	(31)	-0.054	0.035	0.04	-0.07	0.035	-0.005	0.024	0.039	-0.239	-0.281	0.033	0.604
COMSUPER	(32)	-0.008	0.001	-0.006	-0.01	0.007	-0.005	0.031	0.047	-0.005	-0.13	-0.093	0.031
ROBBERY	(33)	0.039	-0.02	-0.04	0.054	0.019	0.004	-0.032	-0.079	0.011	-0.03	0.002	0.003
ASSAULT	(34)	0.065	-0.005	-0.014	-0.024	0.041	0.003	0.044	-0.017	0.014	-0.162	-0.01	-0.053
RAPE	(35)	-0.003	0.03	-0.004	-0.011	-0.006	0.011	0.022	0.003	-0.061	-0.035	0.009	0.069
DEPART	(36)	0.03	0.036	-0.006	0.001	0.014	0.011	-0.008	-0.052	-0.119	0.032	0.073	0.281
MURDER	(37)	0.016	0.01	-0.009	0.005	-0.004	0.006	0.014	0.002	-0.032	-0.024	-0.011	0.087

Appendix A: Correlation Matrix of Variables Included in Analyses (continued)

		13	14	15	16	17	18	19	20	21	22	23	24
MANSLAU	(13)												
BURGLARY	(14)	-0.016											
OTHSEXOF	(15)	-0.039	-0.054										
KIDNAP	(16)	-0.007	-0.009	-0.024									
VEHHOMIC	(17)	-0.012	-0.017	-0.042	-0.007								
OTHERSTR	(18)	-0.019	-0.027	-0.067	-0.012	-0.021							
FIREARM	(19)	-0.014	-0.02	-0.05	-0.009	-0.016	-0.025						
ASSAULT3	(20)	-0.017	-0.023	-0.058	-0.01	-0.018	-0.029	-0.021					
RESBURG	(21)	-0.023	-0.031	-0.079	-0.014	-0.024	-0.039	-0.029	-0.034				
THEFT	(22)	-0.024	-0.033	-0.083	-0.014	-0.026	-0.041	-0.031	-0.035	-0.048			
TMVWP	(23)	-0.013	-0.019	-0.046	-0.008	-0.014	-0.023	-0.017	-0.02	-0.027	-0.028		
STOLPROP	(24)	-0.009	-0.012	-0.031	-0.005	-0.01	-0.015	-0.011	-0.013	-0.018	-0.019	-0.011	
FORGERY	(25)	-0.015	-0.021	-0.054	-0.009	-0.017	-0.027	-0.02	-0.023	-0.031	-0.033	-0.018	-0.012
DRUG	(26)	-0.042	-0.058	-0.146	-0.026	-0.045	-0.073	-0.054	-0.062	-0.085	-0.089	-0.05	-0.033
BELOWDEP	(27)	0.006	-0.001	0.234	-0.017	0.04	-0.01	-0.013	-0.047	-0.049	-0.057	-0.049	-0.051
ABOVEDEP	(28)	-0.036	-0.015	-0.037	-0.008	-0.032	0.064	0.099	0.012	-0.05	0.003	-0.004	-0.002
WEAPON	(29)	0.003	0.006	-0.023	0.003	-0.005	-0.017	0.004	-0.014	-0.007	-0.007	-0.004	0.017
POFFENSES	(30)	0.004	0.004	-0.043	-0.01	0.007	-0.017	0.011	0.01	0.022	0.031	0.011	-0.006
LEVEL	(31)	0.02	0.014	0.086	0.007	0.015	-0.006	-0.007	-0.012	-0.024	-0.055	-0.038	-0.019
COMSUPER	(32)	-0.036	-0.037	0.049	0.014	-0.042	-0.007	-0.005	-0.018	-0.029	-0.015	0	0.011
ROBBERY	(33)	-0.03	-0.044	-0.115	-0.029	-0.034	-0.057	-0.037	-0.045	-0.061	-0.063	-0.037	-0.027
ASSAULT	(34)	-0.033	-0.054	-0.144	-0.024	-0.045	-0.066	-0.051	-0.057	-0.078	-0.083	-0.046	-0.019
RAPE	(35)	-0.012	-0.009	-0.057	-0.01	-0.023	-0.021	-0.011	-0.027	-0.03	-0.031	-0.013	-0.016
DEPART	(36)	0.01	-0.002	-0.037	-0.004	-0.004	0.002	0.031	0.002	-0.003	0.007	0.006	-0.004
MURDER	(37)	0.55	-0.028	-0.071	-0.012	-0.022	-0.035	-0.026	-0.03	-0.041	-0.043	-0.024	-0.016

Appendix A: Correlation Matrix of Variables Included in Analyses (continued)

		25	26	27	28	29	30	31	32	33	34	35	36
FORGERY	(25)												
DRUG	(26)	-0.058											
BELOWDEP	(27)	-0.007	-0.009										
ABOVEDEP	(28)	0.042	0.032										
WEAPON	(29)	-0.004	0	-0.121	-0.025								
POFFENSES	(30)	0.006	0.016	-0.248	-0.106	-0.042							
LEVEL	(31)	-0.027	-0.017	0.683	-0.078	0.095	-0.226						
COMSUPER	(32)	0.004	0.032	0.148	-0.003	0.117	-0.298	0.067					
ROBBERY	(33)	-0.037	-0.11	-0.039	-0.028	-0.03	0.001	0.057	-0.166				
ASSAUT	(34)	-0.047	-0.128	-0.159	0.059	-0.026	-0.081	-0.05	0.103	-0.135			
RAPE	(35)	-0.024	-0.049	-0.036	-0.014	-0.025	-0.04	0.093	0.063	-0.057	-0.068		
DEPART	(36)	-0.001	-0.011	-0.911	0.982	0.054	0.07	0.003	-0.109	0.006	0.049	0.036	
MURDER	(37)	-0.028	-0.076	-0.018	-0.034	-0.001	-0.004	0.063	-0.003	-0.058	-0.067	-0.017	0.014

Appendix B. Interview Questions

ID #________________RESPONDENT_______________

DATE______________ PHONE #____________________

TIME_____________COUNTY____________________

Survey Questions

1). How many years have you been employed by this office?

____

2). What is your personal average caseload? What is the breakdown of your felony cases?

1) Murder_____
2) Robbery_____
3) Burglary_____
4) Assault_____
5) Sex Offenses_____
6) Drug Offenses_____

3). Over the past 5 years, have you seen an increase or decrease in the processing of felony cases in your office?

Increase________Decrease________

In what offenses?

____

4) How many felony cases are plea bargained within your office in a given year? # out of ______ or rough percentage

5) What is the procedure for plea bargained felony cases?

____

____

6) How familiar are you with the creation of the three strikes law in the state?

Very______Somewhat_________

Not Familiar___________

7) How has your office been affected by the three strikes law? If so, how?

____

____

8) Please describe the protocol for handling third strike offenses in you office.

____

____

9) Do you think that the law is good crime control policy? Explain.

____

____

10) What do you think are the policy implications for this law?

____

____

References

Albonetti, C. A. (1991). An integration of theories to explain judicial discretion. *Social Problems, 38*, 247-266.

Albonetti, C. A. (1997). Sentencing under federal sentencing guidelines: Effects of defendant characteristics, guilty pleas, and departures on sentencing outcomes for drug offenses, 1991-1992. *Law and Society Review, 31*, 789-822.

Alschuter, A. (1975). The defense attorney's role in plea bargaining. *The Yale LawJournal, 84(6)*, 1179-1334.

Andenaes, J. (1974). *Punishment and Deterrence*. Ann Arbor: The University of Michigan Press.

Applegate, B.K.; Cullen F.T. Turner, M.G., Sundt, J.L. (1996). Assessing public support for three strikes and you're out laws: Global versus specific attitudes. *Crime and Delinquency, 42(4),* 517-534.

Austin, J. (1996). "The Effect of 'Three Strikes and You're Out' on Corrections." In D. Shichor and D.K. Sechrest(eds.), *Three Strikes and You're Out: Vengeance as Public Policy*. Thousand Oaks, CA: Sage Publications. pp. 155-174.

Austin, J., Clark, J., Hardyman, P., & Henry, D.A. (1999). The impact of 'three strikes and you're out'. *Punishment and Society, 1(2),* 131-162.

Bakeman, R. & Quera, V. (1995). *Analyzing Interaction: Sequential Analysis with SDIS and GSEQ*. New York: Cambridge University Press.

Baldus, D.C., Woodsworth, G. and C. Pulaski. (1985). Comparative Review of death sentences: An empirical study of the Georgia experience. *Journal of Criminal Law and Criminology, 74,* 661-753.

Barnett, A. (1985). Some distribution patterns for Georgia death sentences. *University of California Davis Law Review, 18*, 1327-1374.

Bernstein, I.N., Kelly, W.R. & Doyle, P.A. (1977). Societal reactions to deviants: The case of criminal defendants. *American Sociological Review*. *42,* 743-795.

Blumstein, A. (1996). Interaction of criminological research and public policy. *Journal of Quantitative Criminology, 12(4),* 349-361.

Blumstein, A., Cohen, J., & Farrington, D. (1988). Criminal career research: Its value in criminology. *Criminology, 26*, 57-74.

Blumstein, A., Rivara, F.P., & Rosenfel, R. (2000). The rise and decline of homicide—and why. *Annual Review of Public Health, 21,* 505-541.

Bridges, G. & Crutchfield, R. (1988). Law, social standing, and racial disparities in imprisonment. *Social Forces, 66,* 699-724.

Britt, C.L. (2000). Social context and racial disparities in punishment decisions. *Justice Quarterly, 17(4),* 707-732.

Burnovski, M. & Safra, Z. (1994). Deterrence effects of sequential punishment policies: Should repeat offenders be more severely punished? *International Review of Law and Economics, 14*, 341-350.

Caulkins, J.P. (2001). How large should the strike zone be in 'three strikes and you're out' sentencing laws? *Journal of Quantitative Criminology, 17(3)*, 227-246.

Cheatwood, D. (1993). Capital punishment and the deterrence of violent crime in comparable count. *Criminal Justice Review, 18(2)*, 165-181.

Chiricos, T.G. & Bales, W.D. (1991). Unemployment and punishment: An empirical assessment. *Criminology, 29*, 701-724.

Clancy, K., Bartolomeo, J., Richadson, D., & Wellford, C. (1981). Sentence decision making--the logic of sentence decision and the extent and sources of sentence disparity. *Journal of Criminal Law and Criminology, 72*, 524-554.

Clark, J., Austin, J., &Henry, A. (1997). 'Three Strikes and You're Out': A Review of state legislation. *National Institute of Justice: Research in Brief.* Washington, D.C.: U.S. Department of Justice.

Clark, J., Austin, J., & Henry, A. (1998). 'Three Strikes and You're Out': Are repeat offender laws having their anticipated effects? *Judicature, 81*, 144-149.

Crawford, C. (2000). Gender, race, and habitual offender sentencing in Florida. *Criminology, 38*, 263-280.

Crawford, C., Chiricos, T., & Kleck, G. (1998). Race, racial threat, and sentencing of habitual offenders. *Criminology, 36*, 481-511.

Cullen, F & Gilbert, K. (1982). *Reaffirming Rehabilitation.* Santa Barbara, CA: Anderson Publishing.

Cushman, R.C. (1996). "Effect on the Local Criminal Justice System." In D. Shichor and D.K. Sechrest(eds.), *Three Strikes and You're Out: Vengeance as Public Policy*. Thousand Oaks, CA: Sage Publications. pp.90-113.

D'Alessia, S.J. & Stolzenberg, L. (1995). Impact of sentencing guidelines on jail incarceration in Minnesota. *Criminology, 33(2)* , 282-302.

DiIulio, J. (1991). *No Escape: The Future of American Corrections.* New York: Basic Books.

DiIulio, J. (1995). Arresting ideas: Tougher law enforcement is driving down urban crime. *Policy Review, 74*, 12-16.

Dubber, M. (1995). Recidivist statutes as rational punishment. *Buffalo Law Review, 43*, 689-730.

Durose, M.R., Levin, D.J., & Langan, P.A. (2001). Felony sentences in state courts, 1998. *National Institute of Justice.* Rockville, MD: US Department of Justice.

Eisentein, J., Flemming, R., & Nardulli, P. (1988). *The Contours of Justice: Communities and Their Courts*. Boston: Little Brown.

Ellsworth, P.C. & Gross, S.R. (1994). Hardening of the attitudes: Americans' view on the death penalty. *Journal of Social Issues, 50(2)*, 19-52.

Elvin, J. (1989). Washington state's prison counts drops: will it last? *Corrections Compendium, 14(5)*, 4-7.

Engen, R. L., & Gainey, R. R. (2000). Modeling the effects of legally relevant and extralegal factors under sentencing guidelines: The rules have changed. *Criminology, 38,* 1207-1230.

Feeley, M.M. & Kamin, S. (1996). "The Effect of 'Three Strikes and You're Out' on the Courts: Looking Back to See the Future." In D. Shichor & D.K. Sechrest (eds.), *Three Strikes and You're Out: Vengeance as Public Policy*. Thousand Oaks, CA: Sage Publications. pp. 117-134.

Feld, B. (1987). The juvenile court meets the principle of the offense: Legislative changes in juvenile waiver statues. *The Journal of Criminal Law and Criminology, 78(3)*, 471-533.

Fowler, F. (1993). *Survey Research Methods.* Newbury Park: Sage.

Fox, J. & Radelet, M. (1989). Persistent flaws in econometric studies of the deterrent effect of the death penalty. *Layola of Los Angeles Law Review, 23*, 29-44.

Frost, B. & Rhodes, W.M. (1982). Structuring the exercise of sentencing discretion in the federal courts. *Federal Probation, 46(1)*, 3-13.

Gerber, J. & Englehardt-Greer, S. (1996). "Just and Painful: Attitudes toward Sentencing Criminals." In T. J. Flanagan and D. R. Longmire (eds.), *Americans View Crime and Justice: A National Public Opinion Survey*. Thousands Oaks, CA: Sage Publications. pp. 62-74.

Gibson, L. (1978). Race as a determinate of criminal sentences. *Law and Society Review, 12*, 455-478.

Glass, S. (1997). Anatomy of a policy fraud: The hollow crime bill. *The New Republic*, 22-25.

Gorden, R. (1992). *Basic Interviewing Skills*. Itasca, Illinois: F.E. Peacock Publishers.

Gottfredson, S.D. & Gottfredson, D.M. (1993). Crime control and the criminal career. *California Department of Justice*. Sacramento, CA: Division of Law Enforcement.

Greenwood, P. (June 11, 1995). "Three Strikes Laws Budget Buster of Limited Use." *The Arizona Republic*. E-1.

Greenwood, P., Abrahamse, A., Caulkins, J., Chiesa, J., Model, K., & Klein, S. (1994). Three Strikes and You're Out: Estimated Benefits and Costs of California's New Mandatory Sentencing Law. Santa Monica, CA: Rand.

Griswold, D. (1987). Deviation from sentencing guidelines: The issue of unwarranted disparity. *Journal of Criminal Justice, 15*, 317-329.

Hagan, J. (1974). Extra-legal attributes and criminal sentencing. *Law and Society Review, 8*, 357-383.

Hawkins, D.F. (1987). Beyond anomalies: rethinking the conflict perspective on race and criminal punishment. *Social Forces, 65*, 719-745.

Hogarth, J. (1971). *Sentencing as a Human Process*. Toronto: University of Toronto Press.

Jensen, E.L. & Metsger, L.K. (1994). Test of deterrent effect of legislative waiver on violent juvenile crime. *Crime & Delinquency, 40(1)*, 96-104.

Kalven, H. & Zeisel, H. (1966). *The American Jury*. Boston: Little Brown.

Keil, T. & Vito, G. (1989). Race, homicide severity and application of the death penalty. *Criminology*, *27*, 511-531.

Kempf, K. (1987). Specialization and criminal career. *Criminology, 25*, 9-420.

Kleck, G.C. (1981). Racial discrimination in sentencing. *American Sociological Review, 43,* 783-805.

Klein, S., Petersilia, J., & Turner, S. (1990). Race and imprisonment decisions in California. *Science*, *247*, 812-816.

Klepper, S., Nagin, D., & Tierney, L. (1983). "Discrimination in the Criminal Justice System: A Critical Appraisal of the Literature." In A. Blumstein, J. Cohen, S. Martin, and M. Tonry (eds.), *Research on Sentencing: A Search for Reform*. Washington, D.C.: National Academy Press. pp. 55-128.

Kovandizic, T.V. (2001). The impact of Florida's habitual offender law on crime. *Criminology, 39(1),* 179-203.

Kramer, J. & Steffenmeier, D. (1993). Race and imprisonment decisions. *The Sociological Quarterly*, *34*, 357-376.

Kramer, J. & Ulmer, J. (1996). Sentencing disparity and departures from guidelines. *Justice Quarterly*, *13*, 81-106.

LaFree, G.D. (1985). Adversarial and nonadversarial justice: A comparison of guilty pleas and trial. *Criminology, 23*, 289-312.

LaFree, G.D. (1989). *Rape and Criminal Justice: The Social Constructions of Sexual Assault*. Belmont, CA: Wadsworth.

Lee, G.D. (1995). U.S. sentencing guidelines: Their impact on federal drug offenders. *FBI Law Enforcement Bulletin, 64(5)*, 17-21.

Levin, M.A. (1972). "Urban Politics and Policy Outcomes." In G.F. Cole (ed.), *Criminal Justice: Law and Politics*. Belmont, CA: Wadsworth.

Lizotle, A.J. (1978). Extra-legal factors in Chicago's criminal courts. *Social Problems, 25*, 564-580.

Lynch, R. & Cekola, A. (February 20, 1995). Three strikes law causes juror unease in O.C. *Los Angeles Times*. 1-2

Marvell, T. B. (1995). Sentencing guidelines and prison population growth. *Journal of Criminal Law and Criminology, 85(3)*, 696-709.

Marvell, T.B. & Moody, C. E. (2001). The lethal effects of three-strikes laws. *Journal of Legal Studies, 30,* 89-106.

Maxfield, M. & Babbie, E. (1998). *Research Methods for Criminal Justice and Criminology*. Belmont: CA: Wadsworth.

Maynard, D. (1983). Social order and plea bargaining in the courtroom. *The Sociological Quarterly, 24*, 233-215.

Maynard, D. (1984). *Inside Plea Bargaining*. New York: Plenum Press.

Maynard, D. (1992). Defendants' attributes in plea bargaining: notes on the modeling of sentencing decisions. *Social Problems, 29*, 347-360.

Mays, G. & Houghtalin, M. (1992). Trying juveniles as adults: A note on new Mexico's recent experience. *The Juvenile System Journal, 15*, 814-823.

Meehan, K.E. (2000). California's three-strikes law: The first six years. *Corrections Management Quarterly, 4(4),* 22-33.

Miethe, T. & Moore, C. (1986). Racial differences in criminal processing. *The Sociological Quarterly. 27(2)*, 217-237.

Miller. W. "Life Term for 'strikeouts'." August 14, 1994. *Spokesman Review*. A1.

Moddy, C.E. & Marvell, T.B. (1996). Uncertain timing of innovations in time series: Minnesota sentencing guidelines and jail sentencing: a comment. *Criminology, 34(2)*, 257-267.

Moore, C. & Miethe, T. (1986). Regulated and non-regulated sentencing practices under the Minnesota felony sentencing guidelines. *Law and Society Review, 20*, 253-265.

Myers, M. (1991). "Courts, Prosecution, and Sentencing." In J. F. Sheley (ed.), *Criminology*. New York: West. pp. 359-377.

Myers, M.A. Talarico, S. (1986). The social contexts of racial discrimination in sentencing. *Social Problems, 33*, 236-251.

Myers, M., & Talarico S. (1987). *The Social Contexts of Criminal Sentencing*. New York: Springer-Verlag.

Paternoster, R. (1984). Prosecutorial discretion in requesting the death penalty. *Law and Society Review*, *18,* 437-478.

Pestritto, R.J. (1995). In Defense of Three Strikes: Analyzing the Impact of California's 1994 Anti-Crime Measures. Sacramento, CA: California Assembly Publications.

Petersilia, J., Greenwood, P., & Lavin, M. (1978). *Criminal Careers of Habitual Felons.* National Institute of Law Enforcement and Criminal Justice. U.S. Department of Justice. Washington, D.C.: U.S. Government Printing Office.

Peterson, R. & Hagan, J. (1984). Changing conceptions of race: Towards and account of anomalous findings in sentencing research. *American Sociological Review, 49*, 56-70.

Pruitt, C.R. & Wilson, J.Q. (1983). A longitudinal study on the effect of race on sentencing. *Law and Society Review, 7*, 613-635.

Quinn, T.J. (1992). Delaware: 1992 (SENTAG) Sentencing accountability commission. *Overcrowded Times*. Wilmington: State of Delaware.

Revised Code of Washington 9.92.090. Olympia, WA: Washington State Statute Law Committee.

Revised Code of Washington 9.94A (21). Olympia, WA: Washington State Statute Law Committee.

Revised Code of Washington 9.94A. Persistent Offender Accountability Act. Initiative Measure No. 593. Olympia, WA: Washington State Statute Law Committee.

Roberts, J.V. (1997). "Role of Criminal Record in the Sentencing Process." In M. Tonry (ed.), *Crime and Justice: A Review of Research, Vol. 22*. Chicago: University of Chicago Press. pp. 303-362 .

Ruttenburg, E.A. (1979). Plea Bargaining Analytically—The Nash solution to the Landes Model. *American Journal of Criminal Law, 7*, 323-352.

Sanborn, J. (1994). Certification to criminal court: The important policy questions of how, when, & why. *Crime & Delinquency,40(2)*, 262-281.

Scheingold, S.A. (1995). Politics, public policy, and street crime. *Annals of the American Academy of Political and Social Science, 539*, 155-168.

Schulhofer, S.J. (1993). Rethinking mandatory minimums. *Wake Forest Law Review, 28(2)*, 199-222.

Shane-Du-Bow, S., Brown, A.P., & Olsen, E. (1985). *Sentencing Reform in the united States: History, Content, and Effect*. National Institute of Justice. Washington, D.C.: U.S. Government Printing Office.

Singer, S. (1993). The automatic waiver of juvenile and substantive justice. *Crime & Delinquency, 39,* 253-261.

Spohn, C. (1992). An analysis of the 'Jury Trial Penalty' and its effect on black and white defendants. *The Justice Professional, 7*,93-112.

Spohn, C., & Cederblom, J. (1991). Race and disparities in sentencing: A test of the liberation hypothesis. *Justice Quarterly, 8*, 305-327.

Spohn, C., DeLone, M., & Spears, J. (1998). Race/ethnicity, gender and sentence severity in Dade County, Florida: an examination of the decision to withhold adjudication. *Journal of Crime and Justice, 21(2)*, 111-138.

Spohn, C., Gruhl, J., & Welch, S.(1981-1982). The effect of race on sentencing: a re-examination of the unsettled question. *Law and Society Review, 16*, 72-88.

State of Washington Sentencing Guidelines Commission. (1992). A Statistical Summary of Adult Felony Sentencing: Fiscal Year 1997.

State of Washington v. George W. Manussier, 921 P.2d 473 (1996)

State of Washington v. James M. Thorne, 921 P.2d 514 (1996)

State of Washington v. Paul Rivers, 921 P.2d 495 (1996)

Steffensmeier, D., & Demuth, S. (2000). Ethnicity and sentencing outcomes in U.S. federal courts: Who is punished more harshly? *American Sociological Review, 65*, 705-729.

Steffensmeier, D., Ulmer, J., & Kramer, J. (1998). The interaction of race, gender, and age in criminal sentencing: The punishment cost of being young, black, and male. *Criminology, 36*, 763-797.

Statistical Summary of Adult Felony Sentencing Fiscal Year 2001. (2002). Olympia, WA: Sentencing Guideline Commission, State of Washington.

Stiller, D. (1995). Initiative 593: Washington's voters go swinging. *Gonzaga Law Review, 30*, 435-470.

Stolzenberg, L. & D'Alessio, S.J. (1996). Unintended consequences of linking sentencing guidelines to prison populations: A reply to Moddy and Marvell. *Criminology, 32(2)*, 269-279.

Taifa, N. (1995). Symposium: Violent crime control and law enforcement act of 1994, three strikes and you're out-mandatory life imprisonment for third time felons. *Dayton Law Review, 20*, 717-725.

Talarico, S.M. (1979). Judicial decisions and sanction patterns in criminal justice. *Journal of Criminal Law and Criminology, 70(1)*, 117-124.

Tonry, M. (1992). "Mandatory Penalties." In M. Tonry and N. Morris (eds.), *Crime and Justice: A Review of Research, Vol. 16*. Chicago: University of Chicago Press. pp. 243-274.

Tonry, M. (1995). *Malign Neglect: Race, Crime and Punishment in America*. New York: Oxford University Press.

Tonry, M. (1996). *Sentencing Matters*. New York: Oxford University Press.

Uhlman, T. M. & Walker, N. D. (1979). Plea is no bargain--the impact of case disposition on sentencing. *Social Science Quarterly,60(2)*, 218-234.

Uhlman, T.M. & Walker, J.D. (1980). He takes some of my time, I take some of his! *Law and Society Review, 14*, 323-341.

Ulmer, J.T. (1997). *Social Worlds of Sentencing: Court Communities Under Sentencing Guidelines.* Albany: State University of New York Press.

Ulmer, J.T. (2000). The rules have changed-so proceed with caution: A comment on Engen and Gainey's method for modeling sentencing outcomes under guidelines. *Criminology, 38*(4), 1231-1243.

Unnever, J. & Hembroff, L. (1987). The prediction for racial/ethnic sentencing disparities. *Journal of Research in Crime and Delinquency, 25*, 530-82.

von Hirsch, A. (1994). Symposium on sentencing guidelines and guidance. *Criminal Justice Ethics, 13(1)*, 3-66.

von Hirsch, A. & Greene, J.(1993). When should reformers support creation of sentencing guidelines? *Wake Forest Law Review, 28(2)*, 329-343.

Walsh, A. (1987). The sexual stratification hypothesis and sexual assault in light of the changing conceptions of race. *Criminology, 25*, 153-173.

Walsh, A. (1990). Standing trial versus copping a plea: Is there a penalty? *Journal of Contemporary Criminal Justice, 8(4)*, 226-253.

Welch, S, Gruhl, J., & Spohn, C. (1984). The influence of alternative measures of prior record. *Criminology, 22*, 214-227.

Wolfgang, M. R. Figlio, & Sellin, T. (1972). *Delinquency in a Birth Cohort.* Chicago: University of Chicago Press.

Zatz, M.S. (1984). Race, ethnicity, and determinate sentencing: a new dimension to an old controversy. *Criminology,22*, 147-171.

Zatz, M. S. (1986). The changing forms of racial/ethnic biases in sentencing. *Journal of Research in Crime and Delinquency,24*, 69-92.

Zatz, M.S. (1987). The changing forms of racial/ethnic biases in sentencing. *Journal of Research in Crime and Delinquency,24*, 69-92.

Zimbardo, P. (1994). Transforming California's Prisons Into Expensive Old Age Homes for Felons: Enormous Hidden Costs and Consequences for California's Taxpayers. San Francisco: Center on Juvenile and Criminal Justice.

Zimring, F. E., & Hawkins, G. (1991). The Scale of Imprisonment. Chicago: University of Chicago Press.

Zimring, F. E., Hawkins, G., & Kamin, S. (2001). *Punishment and Democracy: Three strikes and You're Out in California.* New York: Oxford University Press.

Zimring, F.E. (1971). *Perspectives on deterrence.* Washington, DC: U.S. Government Printing Office.

Index